BRITISH MUSEUM

OCCASIONAL PAPER NUMBER 126

HUMPHREY COLE
MINT, MEASUREMENT AND MAPS IN ELIZABETHAN ENGLAND

Edited by Silke Ackermann

BRITISH MUSEUM OCCASIONAL PAPERS

Publishers: The British Museum
Great Russell Street
London WC1B 3DG

Production Editor: Josephine Turquet

Distributors: British Museum Press
46 Bloomsbury Street
London WC1B 3QQ

Occasional Paper No. 126, 1998

Humphrey Cole: Mint, Measurement and Maps
Silke Ackermann

ISBN 0 86159 126 7
ISSN 0142 4815

Front cover: Humphrey Cole's map of Palestine of 1572 (catalogue no. 27) with the astrolabe of 1574 (catalogue no. 19) and two gold coins (catalogue no. 28 (1 and 4) superimposed.

For a complete catalogue giving information on the full range of available Occasional Papers please write to:
The Marketing Assistant
British Museum Press
46 Bloomsbury Street
London WC1B 3QQ

Printed and bound in the UK by The Chameleon Press Limited

CONTENTS

ESSAYS

CATALOGUES

Preface

The use of scientific instruments as evidence for studies in the history of science has increased significantly in recent years. With this development have come changes in the role the instruments themselves play in these studies. Many entered the earlier collections as examples of fine medieval or Renaissance metalwork and the artistry and craftsmanship involved in their production was of primary interest. Later, the scientific qualities of the instruments were studied and they were related to developing intellectual ideas of their times. More recently still, it has been possible to consider the role of instruments in their relationship to the social and economic history of their times such as the enclosure of land, map-making and the expansion of trade.

The first English instrument maker known by name, Humphrey Cole, was active at a time when England's wealth was greatly increasing and the need for accurate measurement was being felt. He was by no means an isolated figure, and a group of makers appeared nearly simultaneously in late sixteenth-century Elizabethan England. Cole did not confine his activities to his instrument-making skills but was also employed as an engraver to the Royal Mint, thereby playing a role in creating the money reflecting the nation's wealth which ultimately funded his instrument enterprise. The techniques involved in manufacture seem to have been learned from Low Country practitioners. One thing is clear: the English makers did not take long to teach and the profession was well-established by the beginning of the seventeenth century. The earliest instruments are superbly well made and, even if difficult to find because of their scarcity, are a pleasure to study.

Museums in the United Kingdom amassed particularly fine collections of early scientific instruments and the British Museum acquired these earliest of all. Its foundation collection of 1753 included the Sloane astrolabe of the late thirteenth century and the first Cole instrument, an astrolabe dated 1574, was acquired in 1857. Since then, the Science Museum, London, National Maritime Museum, Greenwich, Museum of the History of Science, Oxford, Whipple Museum of the History of Science, Cambridge and the National Museums of Scotland in Edinburgh have employed specialists who have collected vigorously; all have lent to this exhibition. Furthermore, the University of St. Andrews, the Royal Artillery Historical Trust, the British Library, and a private collector have also made generous loans. The Museé de la Vie Wallonne, Liège, Museo di Storia della Scienza, Florence, and Kunstgewerbemuseum, Berlin have provided photographs of their instruments to be included in the catalogue. To all these we offer our most grateful thanks. Additionally curators of two British Museum Departments, Medieval and Later Antiquities and Coins and Medals are to be congratulated on developing the concept of the exhibition and mounting it.

The exhibition, the first of its kind, and this catalogue, could not have been produced without outside funding, and for this, the Scientific Instrument Research Fund, the British Museum Society and the Townley Group came to the rescue at a time when other sources of finance were in short supply. They too deserve warm thanks.

R.G.W. Anderson — Director

ESSAYS

THE

MATHEMATICAL IEVVEL,

Shewing the making, and most excellent vse of a singuler Instrument so called: in that it performeth with wonderfull dexteritie, whatsoeuer is to be done, either by Quadrant, Ship, Circle, Cylinder, Ring, Dyall, Horoscope, Astrolabe, Sphere, Globe, or any such like heretofore deuised: yea or by most Tables commonly extant: and that generally to all places from Pole to Pole.

The vse of which Iewel, is so aboundant and ample, that it leadeth any man practising thereon, the direct pathway (from the first steppe to the last) through the whole Artes of Astronomy, Cosmography, Geography, Topography, Nauigation, Longitudes of Regions, Dyalling, Sphericall triangles, Setting figures; and briefely of whatsoeuer concerneth the Globe or Sphere: with great and incredible speede, plainenesse, facillitie, and pleasure:

The most part newly founde out by the Author; Compiled and published for the furtherance, as well of Gentlemen and others desirous of speculatiue knowledge, and priuate practise: as also for the furnishing of such worthy mindes, Nauigators, and traueylers, that pretend long voyages or new discoueries: By Iohn Blagraue of Reading Gentleman and well willer to the Mathematickes; who hath cut all the prints or pictures of the whole worke with his owne hands. 1585.

gabrielharuey. 1585.

Imprinted at London by Walter Venge, dwelling in Fleetelane ouer against the Maiden head.

Figure 1 *A handwritten note by Gabriel Harvey (c. 1550-1630) the Cambridge poet, on his copy of John Blagrave's* The Mathematical Jewel *(1585), referring to Kynvyn and Cole (British Library c.60.o.7). Reproduced by kind permission of the British Library.*

Queen Elizabeth's Instrument Makers

G.L'E. Turner

The development of the precision scientific instrument trade in London was the direct result of two far-reaching events in the fifteenth century. The first was the invention, around 1460, of printing with movable type, together with the increased availability of paper, as paper mills were opened for the first time in northern Europe. Engraving on metal was not a new phenomenon, but the printed image became more readily available, and was used for book illustration. More significantly, it was used in the production of maps, for which the demand became urgent, following the discovery in 1492 of the American continent. This created across Europe an economic imperative to exploit the trading and colonizing potential of the New World. An urgent demand arose not only for maps and charts, but also for the equipment to be used in surveying and mapping, and for instruments to aid deep-sea navigation.

Professional surveying consists of plotting the position of certain landmarks on the surface of the Earth for the purpose of producing a graphic representation of the area, accurately reduced to scale. The need to measure land developed as soon as communities became settled. The Flemish *landmeeter* (a word that still means surveyor) was in existence as early as the twelfth century, for in 1190 this description was added to a practitioner's name: Bernoldo Landmetra. In 1282, Johannes Landmetere is referred to as Geometricus and Agrimensor.

Surveys, as understood from the seventeenth century onwards, have depended on linear and angular measurements. Until the sixteenth century, however, surveying was a simple process carried out with direct measure of length, mainly by using poles and ropes. The trained eye played a part, and simple calculations were involved. Surveying books from the first half of the sixteenth century deal largely with carrying out audits and valuations, and only begin to touch on land measurement proper. Richard Benese was a Canon of the Augustinian Priory of Merton who published, in 1537, the earliest English text on geometrical surveying and area measurement. The title is: *This Boke sheweth the Maner of Measuring all maner of Lands...*, and there Benese recommends the use of a wooden rod the length of a perch (16½ feet), and a cord of five perches in length. (An acre measures 40 perches in length and 4 in breadth). Thus at that time only rudimentary tools and not instruments were available to the surveyor in the field.

During the first half of the sixteenth century the scene was being set for the development of surveying into a profession, requiring increasing skill and accuracy, and also the use of instruments devised to make angular measurements. Surveying was professionalized alongside, and to a certain extent as a result of, the development of deep-sea navigation and the growing military skills of fortification and siege associated with the use of artillery. The accurate determination of position, both at sea and on land, became of increasing economic importance as ships left the security of coastal waters, and as new tracts of unexplored territory were discovered. One of the major activities of a surveyor is levelling. Water running from high ground to sea level causes problems in flat coastal areas, as in the Low Countries and the English Fens. It was the surveyor's task to devise waterways, dikes, and locks to rescue land for agriculture to feed an increasing population, and hence promote economic gain.

The disintegration of the medieval pattern of land tenure led to the establishment of a much higher proportion of individual ownership, and so to the need for more accurate definition of boundaries. As a result of these needs the art of map-making grew rapidly in importance at a time when the necessary skills of engraving and printing were available, most notably in the Low Countries. The engraver of copper-plate illustrations could also learn to make maps, and to divide the circle on brass instruments for the use of the surveyor and the seaman. Another important requirement, both for instrument makers and for those who practised surveying and navigation, was mathematical knowledge. As with printing and engraving, mathematics, in particular in the practical applications, was developed on the Continent of Europe by such notable scholars as Martin Waldseemüller (1470–*c.* 1518) in Lorraine, and Gemma Frisius (1508–1555) at Louvain. During the mid-sixteenth century, John Dee (1527–1608), a founder Fellow of Trinity College, Cambridge, spent three years studying in Paris, Brussels, and Louvain, and on his return home he pioneered the provision of textbooks and translations of Continental practice in English.

At much the same time, in 1543, the highly influential work by Robert Recorde, *The Ground of Artes Teaching the Worke and practise of Arithmetike* was published, which, running through 28 editions in the next 150 years, introduced pen reckoning and the use of arabic numerals to a wide public. Before the new, angular measuring techniques could be satisfactorily imported from the Continent, a prior requirement was a knowledge of arithmetic: arabic had to replace roman numerals. In the Exchequer Records, a stronghold of tradition, arabic numerals were first used at the end of the sixteenth century, and roman did not disappear for another 60 years. Accounts were done by using ruled boards or cloths, and casting-counters; hence the phrase: to cast one's accounts. Recorde, a Fellow of All Souls College, Oxford in 1531, and the first to use the equality symbol =, may be regarded as the founder of English mathematics, since his text-books opened the way to self-education for the new class of technicians. He was also the founder of the English school of mathematical practitioners, among whom were later numbered many of the great London instrument makers.

The English mechanician, Cyprian Lucar (fl.1564-1590), who was educated at Winchester College and New College, Oxford, published at London in 1590 his *Treatise named Lucar Solace*, where he illustrated the instruments in common use during the late sixteenth century. His selection is soon confirmed by John Norden in *The Surveyors Dialogue* of 1607. The illustration in Lucar's book shows a plane table with frame to hold the paper and an alidade or ruler, a chain, a square, and a pair of compasses. Rods and cords for direct measurement were in use throughout the century, but the metal chain, an obvious - though expensive - improvement on the cord because it was not subject to variation in length, was first referred to by Conrad von Ulm in a book he published at Strasbourg in 1579. The length of the chain was related to various local measures, and the Gresham Professor, Edmund Gunter proposed a decimal chain of 100 links in 1620. Also used for direct measurement of length, though not shown by Lucar, was the waywiser. A dial recorded the revolution of the wheels of a carriage, and soon a hand-propelled measuring wheel, also called a waywiser or a perambulator, came into use in the seventeenth century, and continues to be used today.

The plane table was the most ubiquitous of sixteenth-century surveying instruments, being practical and easy to use in the field. It is a board with paper held down on it, surmounted by an alidade or ruler with sights at each end. By aligning the sights with topographical features and marking the line of view by pencil along the side of the alidade, the plan is simply made. The plane table was, however, despised by those with mathematical knowledge. Thomas Digges, in the 1591 edition of his father's book, *Pantometria*, described it as 'an Instrument onely for the ignorante and unlearned, that haue no knowledge of Noumbers'. Throughout the sixteenth century mathematicians were working on versions of an instrument for surveying that eventually became the theodolite. The first man to design what was recognizably an altazimuth theodolite was Martin Waldseemüller, who produced in Lorraine not only world maps, but also detailed maps of his own area of the upper Rhine. In the 1512 edition of the *Margarita Philosophica* of Gregor Reisch, which is a philosophical and scientific compendium, there was included a section on architecture and perspective by Waldseemüller that depicted an instrument called the 'Polimetrum', which contained the two essential devices for the simultaneous measurement of horizontal and vertical angles.

Leonard Digges (d.1571?) of University College, Oxford, and his son, Thomas (d.1595) of Queens' College, Cambridge, were the authors of two influential texts on mathematical surveying, published in the second half of the sixteenth century. In the first of these, entitled *Tectonicon*, and published at London in 1556, Leonard described those for whom the book was intended as 'Surveyors, Landmeaters, Ioyners, Carpenters and Masons'. As well as providing tables to help those who used measuring cords, he recommends three instruments: the carpenter's ruler, the carpenter's square, and a version of the cross-staff. It was, however, in his posthumously published *A Geometrical Practice Named Pantometria* (1571), completed by his son, that Digges introduced instruments for the specialist surveyor. He described three instruments that could be combined to form what he called a 'topographicall instrument'. These were: a vertical quadrant with shadow square that was intended to measure heights; a square with inscribed quadrant and alidade, mounted on a staff; and a circular plate divided into degrees with a centrally mounted alidade, to which Digges gave the name 'theodelitus'. The combination was, in effect, an altazimuth theodolite, while the 'theodelitus' by itself was the simple theodolite. An astrolabe could be used for measuring horizontal or vertical angles, and one can see that the theodolite, which combines the means to make both measurements, can be said to derive from the astrolabe. Sixteenth-century astrolabes often incorporate a magnetic compass. Aaron

Rathborne, in his book called *The Surveyor*, published in 1616, lists the following instruments: the plane table; the altazimuth theodolite; the circumferentor; the simple theodolite; and a chain. This list reflects the gradual acceptance during the course of the sixteenth century of versions of the more elaborate mathematical instruments that had at first been regarded as too complex by the working surveyor.

To summarize, the basic techniques of surveying, then as now, comprise: measuring angles, and the length of a baseline. After sighting prominent features with the angle-measuring instrument at one and then the other end of the baseline, and knowing its length, it is a simple matter to calculate the distance of a feature by the theorem of similar triangles. It is also possible to draw a plan or map to scale. Other requirements are to measure heights and depths and distance, to ascertain the orientation, and to achieve a level. Surveying is an intensely practical activity, so that the development of instruments for use by surveyors was always conditioned by factors such as compactness, and speed and ease of use. The theory was established by the early seventeenth century and changed little over the next 300 years. It was the instruments that evolved, becoming more accurate and efficient, and better adapted to differing conditions.

Much the same may be said about navigation at sea. While in coastal waters, the seaman relied on experience, a lead line, and a magnetic compass. Crossing the Atlantic was a completely different matter, for experience was very hardly gained, and quite definitely instruments were required when out of sight of land, birds, and other tell-tale features. He still needed the lead, log-line, and magnetic compass, but also a quadrant, a forestaff, a sand-glass, charts, and a good knowledge of the star map. Two books on navigational techniques from the end of the Elizabethan period deserve special mention. One is William Barlow's *The Navigators Supply* of 1597. Barlow (fl. 1564-1625) was a graduate of Balliol College, Oxford, churchman at Winchester and then chaplain to Prince Henry, son of James I. Barlow abhorred the sea, but through his knowledge of mathematics, and by talking with seamen, he learnt of what was needed and proceeded to invent instruments. He improved the magnetic compass, and invented or improved the variation compass, the pantometer, the hemisphere, the traverse board, and what he called the Traveller's Jewel. The Jewel was a combination of variation compass and equinoctial sundial. There was an advertisement on his title page, just above the engraving of the Traveller's Jewel which ran:

> If any man desire more ample instruction concerning the vse of these instruments, hee may repayre vnto Iohn Goodwin dwellinge in Bucklersburye teacher of the grownds of these artes. The instruments are made by Charles Whitwell, over agaynste Essex howse, maker of all sortes of mathematicall instruments, and the graver of these portraytures [that is to say, the eight engravings in the book].

David Waters, in his masterly history of navigation, has written of Edward Wright: 'his book set the seal on the supremacy of the English in the theory and practice of the art of navigation at the end of the sixteenth century'. Wright is even mentioned in the *Dictionary of National Biography*, where it says he effected a revolution in the science of navigation. Yet another Cambridge mathematician, who became a fellow of his college, Caius, Wright was brought into the Queen's service as a result of the Armada, and travelled on naval ships to gain practical experience. The result was *Certaine Errors in Navigation, arising either of the ordinarie erroneous making or using of the sea Chart, Compasses, Crosse staffe, and Table of declination of the Sunne, and fixed Starres detected and corrected*, published in 1599. Here Wright provided a most thorough mathematical treatment of errors in measurements and in the practices of seamen.

Printers and copper-plate engravers from Flanders strongly influenced English practice. Robert Recorde's *The Ground of Artes* (1543) was printed by Reynor Wolfe, who left his native Drenthe in the north of the Netherlands to settle in London in 1533. Even 50 years later it was difficult to find an English printer who could set up a mathematical work correctly. Throughout the sixteenth century the English were indebted to the Continent, and especially to the Netherlands, north and south, for the skills of printing, of engraving book illustrations, maps, and instruments, and for surveying techniques. All these activities are melded together in the work of Christopher Saxton (d.1596), who was obliged to farm out his engraving needs to several men to hasten the production of engraved maps. His *An Atlas of England and Wales*, published at London in 1579, contains 34 maps, 23 of them bearing the engraver's name. There are seven different signatures, four of them by Flemings, and three by Englishmen. The English are: Augustine Ryther (4 maps), Francis Scatter (2), and Nicholas Reynolds (1). Ryther was to become a leading instrument maker. The migration of skilled men increased during the middle of the century when the grip of Spanish religious persecution was tightening on the Netherlands, finally to result in the Revolt which broke out in 1564.

The major influence on sixteenth-century instrument design, and on map, chart, and globe making, came from Gemma Frisius of Louvain University, and Gerard Mercator (1512-1594), the great cartographer. It is, therefore, not surprising that from the Louvain area arrived the man who can be regarded as the first to establish the scientific instrument-making trade in England. Thomas Gemini (*c.*1510-1562) came from the Low Countries, and as an engraver made his reputation with his plates for his own printing of the *Anatomy* of Vesalius, issued in London in 1545. This earned him an annuity of £10 from Henry VIII. At Blackfriars, he carried on the business of printer and illustrator, map-engraver, and mathematical instrument-maker. An astrolabe by him is in a Belgium museum bearing the arms of the Duke of Northumberland and of King Edward VI. It is dated 1552. In 1555 Gemini printed the *Prognostications* of Leonard Digges, and in the following year, Digges' *A Boke Named Tectonicon.* It was said there that the instruments could be obtained from Gemini. Another astrolabe was made for Queen Elizabeth. This is dated 1559, and is engraved with the queen's name and the royal arms. It is to be seen in the Museum of the History of Science, Oxford. It came to Oxford through John Greaves (1602-1652), Gresham Professor and later Savilian Professor of Astronomy at Oxford from 1643 to 1648. Greaves took the astrolabe on his journey to the Levant during 1637-1640, and used it to determine the latitude of Rhodes. He measured the pyramids, but seems not to have found God's yard.

A key factor in the establishment of the instrument-making trade in London was to find a way in which it could become grafted on to the existing guild structure. The City of London guilds were medieval, and, by the sixteenth century, what are known as the Twelve Great Livery Companies had emerged as leaders. To learn a craft and to practise it meant that an apprenticeship had to be served, and the arrangement properly recorded and approved by a City Company. Practising a new craft, mathematical instrument makers had to find a company as best they might; one was to join a father's company, whichever it might be, under the patrimony arrangement. New companies were formed, of course: the Spectacle-Makers in 1629, the Clockmakers in 1631. But the mathematical instrument-makers were captured to a great and surprising extent by one of the Twelve Great Livery Companies, the Grocers. Once a master-apprentice succession was established, the instrument makers remained in the Company, and so a school was built up. This has been fully explored by Joyce Brown in her book on *Mathematical Instrument Makers in the Grocers' Company* (1979).

Following a Privy Council recommendation that citizens should be instructed in military matters, Thomas Hood, a mathematician from Trinity College, Cambridge, was appointed the first Thomas Smith lecturer in mathematics in the City of London, in 1582. Hood published in 1598 his *The Making and Vse of the Geometrical Instrument called a Sector.* There are three sectors of this same type, two, both dated 1597, by Robert Beckit and Charles Whitwell, and one undated by James Kynvyn. These London sectors pre-date the publication in 1606 of Galileo's work on the sector. As for Robert Beckit himself, little is known except that he engraved five maps for the London 1598 edition of Van Linschoten's *Discourse of Voyages into ye East & West Indies.* The Cambridge poet, Gabriel Harvey (*c.*1550-1630), in a note on his copy of John Blagrave's *The Mathematical Jewel* (1585), tells us more about Kynvyn (Figure 1):

> James Kynvyn of London, near Powles. A fine workman & mie kinde frend: first commended vnto me bie M. Digges & M. Blagrave himself... He & old Humfrie Cole, mie mathematical mechanicians

A representative group of 20 English Elizabethan instruments are, by a happy accident of history, to be found in Florence. Sir Robert Dudley (1574-1649), son of the Earl of Leicester, left England in 1606 to settle in Florence. Dudley had commanded a man-of-war at the sack of Cadiz in 1596, and was knighted after the battle. He settled in Florence at the court of the Medici, and there planned the fortification of the port of Leghorn, and worked on naval architecture. His three-volume *Dell' Arcano del Mare* is a masterpiece. The English-made instruments he brought with him remain in the Museo di Storia della Scienza. In this time capsule, the makers represented include: Humfrey Cole, James Kynvyn, Augustine Ryther, and Charles Whitwell, who was apprenticed to Ryther.

Ryther was an engraver of distinction, and signed some of his maps 'Augustinus Ryther Anglus', as was customary to make the distinction from the Flemish engravers. His earliest signed products are the maps dated 1576, engraved for Christopher Saxton. A pack of playing cards is also attributed to him. In 1582, Ryther took as his apprentice for nine years Charles Whitwell (d.1611), who obtained his freedom of the Grocers' Company in 1590. Hood advertised on the title page of his book on the *Sector* that 'the

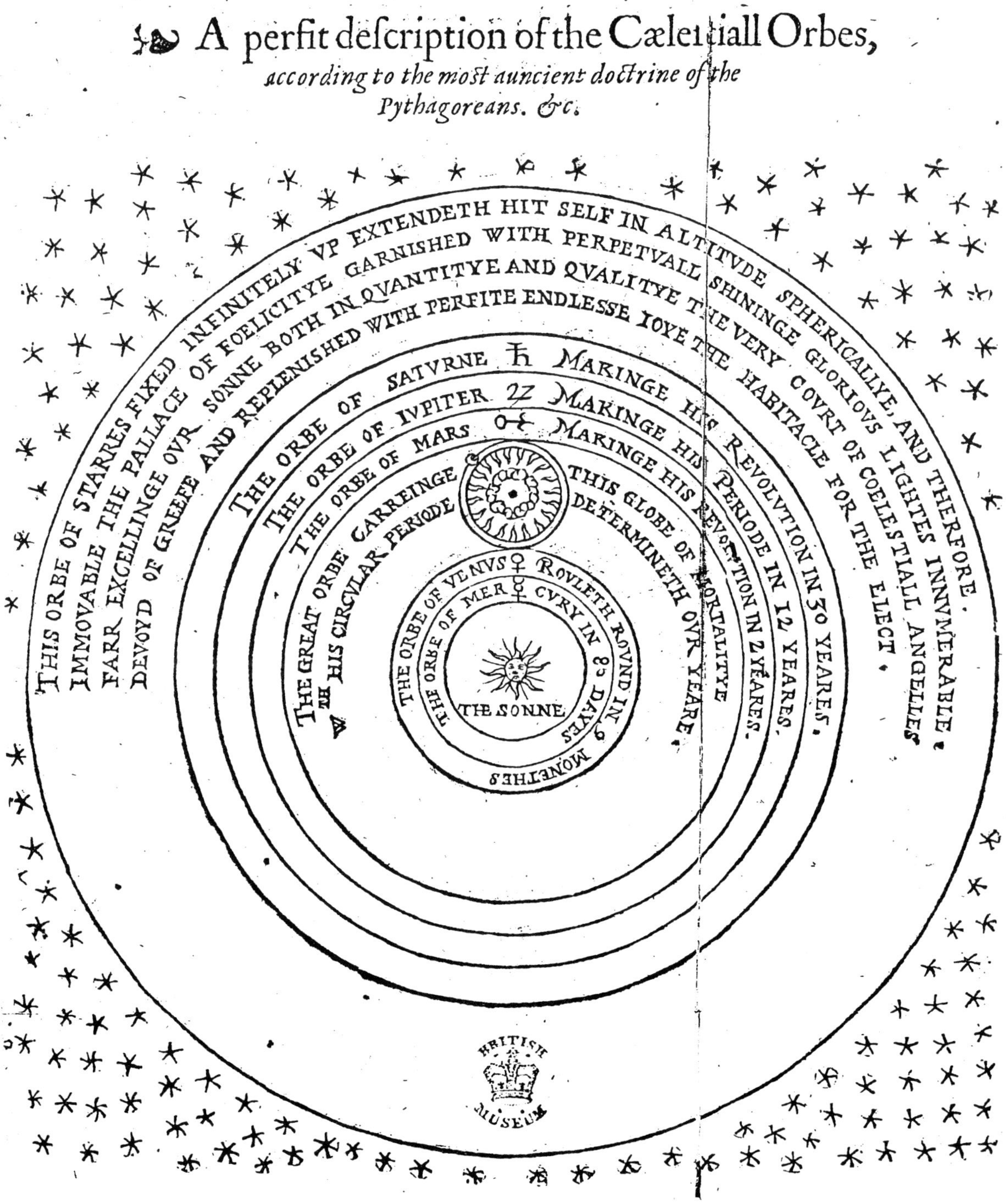

Figure 2 This cosmographical diagram was published in 1576 by Thomas Digges (c. 1543-1593) in his A Perfit Description of the Caelestiall Orbes *that he added to an edition of his late father's* A Prognostication of Right Good Effect, *which was first published in 1555. This diagram is the first representation in English of the Copernican world system, showing an infinity of stars. The engraving is attributed to Humfrey Cole by G.L'E. Turner (British Library 718.g.52). Reproduced by kind permission of the British Library.*

instrument is made by Charles Whitwell, dwelling without Temple Barre against St Clements Church'. Whitwell engraved the illustrations for Hood's book, and did the same service for other authors. There are eight men among his known apprentices, the most famous being the distinguished Elias Allen (d.1655), who became free of the Grocers' in 1612 after serving for nine years. With Allen, the London trade in scientific instruments was well and truly established.

But without any doubt, the English originator of the London scientific instrument trade, and its foremost practitioner in the sixteenth century was 'old Humfrie Cole'. Cole (*c.* 1530-1591) came from the north of England, probably Yorkshire, and was employed in the Royal Mint, in the office of Sinker. He supplied some basic information about himself on the cartouche of his map of the Holy Land: 'GRAVEN BI HUMFRAY COLE GOLDSMITH A ENGLISH MAN BORN IN Y NORTH AND PEARTAYNING TO Y^E^ MINT IN THE TOWER. 1572'. The map was commissioned by Richard Jugge (1547-1577), the printer and publisher of Bibles, to illustrate the 1572 edition of the *Bishops' Bible*. This was undertaken on the initiative of Matthew Parker, Archbishop of Canterbury, in 1563, to improve the authorized *Great Bible*, and to challenge the popularity of the Calvinistic *Genevan Bible*. Another printing commission undertaken by Cole came from Thomas Digges, who republished his father's *A Prognostication of Right Good Effect* (London, 1576), to which he added his own *A Perfit Description of the Caelestiall Orbes*. This was the first discussion in English of the Copernican world system. The heavens were no longer thought of as bounded by the sphere of the fixed stars. On the contrary, the stars stretched out to infinity. A diagram to illustrate this novel view was printed (Figure 2), and Humfrey Cole has been identified for the first time as the engraver by the present writer.

Cole's skill as an engraver is manifest from his maps, illustrations, and instruments. He was also knowledgeable about mining and minerals. In this capacity, he was closely involved in the setting up of the Company of Mineral and Battery Works, which, together with the Company of Mines Royal, was granted a Royal Charter in 1568. Brass had traditionally been imported from the Continent, but growing demand for brass and bronze gave the impetus to promote English manufacture. This in its turn meant that German craftsmen had to be recruited to teach Englishmen metal-working skills and prospecting for ores.

From his work at the Mint, and his knowledge of metal-working, Humfrey Cole moved naturally into mathematical instrument making. He undertook to supply all the instruments described in the 1571 edition of Digges' *Pantometria*. The 26 instruments by him that have survived show the variety of his production. His masterpiece must surely be the large, two-foot diameter astrolabe, dated 1575, in the possession of the University of St. Andrews, Scotland. This resembles in several respects the Gemini astrolabe made for Queen Elizabeth I, both instruments having on the back a horizontal projection of the sphere derived from the planisphere of Gemma Frisius. As would be expected, Cole strongly influenced later makers. This is shown through comparison of Cole's two theodolites with those by Ryther and Kynvyn. It is also instructive to compare pocket dials by Cole, Ryther, Kynvyn, Whitwell and Elias Allen. In one respect, however, Cole differed from others in this group, in that he was free of the Goldsmiths' Company, because of his connection with the Mint, not of the Grocers' Company.

The scientific instruments that have survived from the sixteenth century are, predominantly, those made of metal, and those that belonged to people of status, or to scholars. This is not always true, but instruments of wood were inevitably regarded as more expendable, while instruments used in the field or at sea had a poorer chance of survival than those used in the study. Nevertheless, we know that there was a considerable production of wooden instruments, particularly for use by surveyors and seamen. An author on practical surveying, Edward Worsop, published as a supplement to his book in 1582, an advertisement for a number of London instrument makers, giving the reason: 'many that would provide [*ie.* obtain] such things, knowe not where to have them'. His list includes some makers of metal instruments (including Humfrey Cole), and three for wooden instruments: John Reade of Hosier Lane, James Lockerson of Dowgate, and John Reynolds of Tower Hill.

By 1600, the number of men trained as engravers had increased, and workshops had grown in number and size. Instruments became more complex and varied, with competition in producing new designs to catch attention and to compete with rivals. Earlier, craftsmen had worked in collaboration with the scholar-inventor; now they were to become capable of independent invention. Instruments for astronomy, time-telling, navigation, and surveying were created for economic reasons. There was, too a market for wealthy men interested in scientific matters, and elaborately embellished instruments were provided for them. But this group is more obviously catered for by the products of the leading Continental makers rather than the English, whose instruments are austerely functional.

Bibliography

Bennett, J.A., 'Geometry and Surveying in Early-Seventeenth-Century England', *Annals of Science* 48 (1991), pp. 345-354.

Brown, J., *Mathematical Instrument-Makers in the Grocers' Company 1688-1830* (London 1979).

Brown, J., 'Guild Organization and the Instrument-Making Trade, 1550-1830', *Annals of Science* 36 (1979), pp. 1-34.

Johnston, S.A., 'Mathematical Practitioners and Instruments in Elizabethan England', *Annals of Science*, 48 (1991), 319-344.

Karrow, R.W., Jr., *Mapmakers of the Sixteenth Century and their Maps* (Chicago, Newberry Library, 1993).

Richeson, A.W., *English Land Measuring to 1800: Instruments and Practice* (Cambridge, Mass., 1966).

Roche, J.J., 'The Radius Astronomicus in England', *Annals of Science* 38 (1981), pp. 1-32.

Taylor, E.G.R., *The Mathematical Practitioners of Tudor and Stuart England* (Cambridge 1954).

Turner, Gerard L'E., *Scientific Instruments and Experimental Philosophy 1550-1850* (Aldershot: Variorum 1991).

Turner, Gerard L'E., 'Mathematical Instrument-Making in London in the Sixteenth Century', *English Map-Making 1500-1650: Historical Essays*, ed. S. Tyacke (London 1983), chapter 7.

Ward, F.A.B., *A Catalogue of European Scientific Instruments in the Department of Medieval and Later Antiquities of the British Museum* (London 1981).

Waters, D.W., *The Art of Navigation in England in Elizabethan and Early Stuart Times* (London 1958).

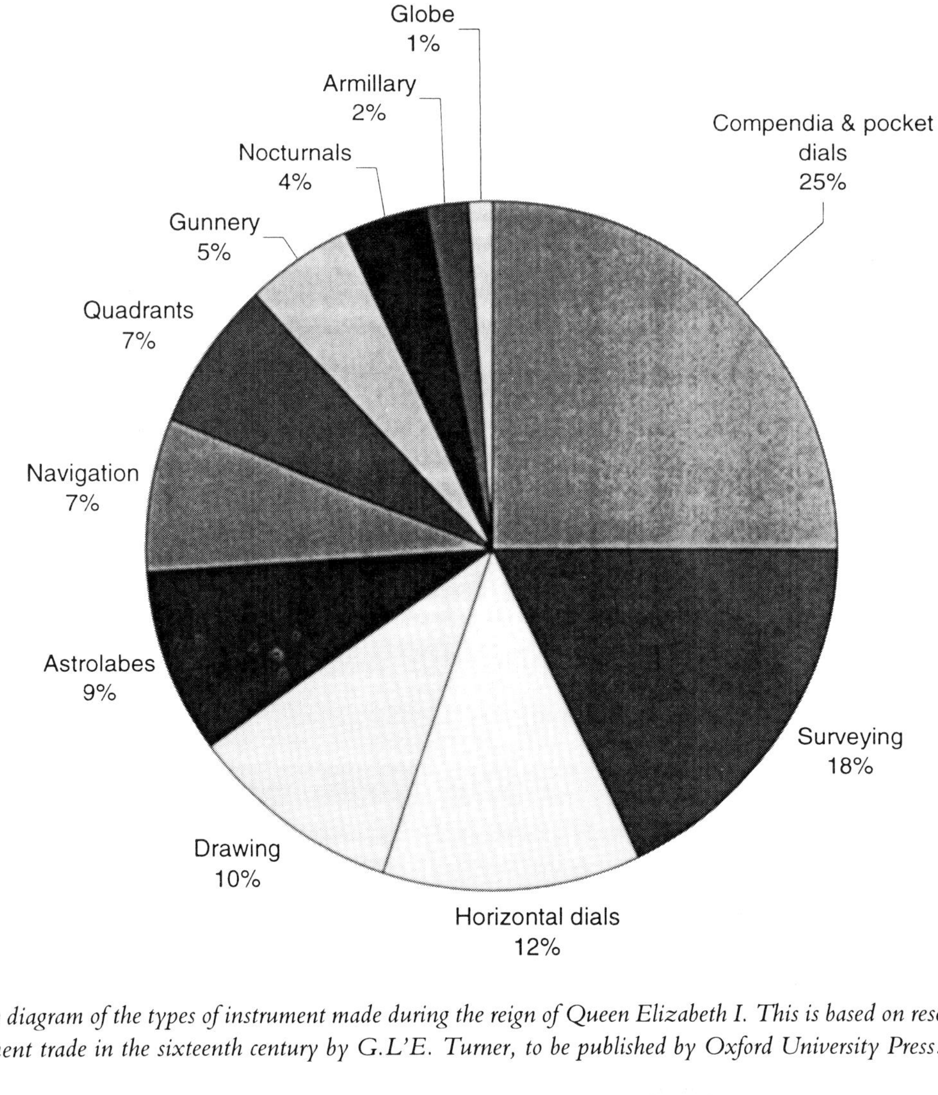

Figure 3 A pie diagram of the types of instrument made during the reign of Queen Elizabeth I. This is based on research into the London scientific instrument trade in the sixteenth century by G.L'E. Turner, to be published by Oxford University Press.

Mapmaking in Humphrey Cole's England

Peter Barber

Humphrey Cole grew up in a period of renewed interest in mapping in England.[1] The theories and practice of mapping developed in southern Germany from the late fifteenth century and transmitted to England through individuals such as Henry VIII's court astronomer, Nicolaus Kratzer; the more general awakening of interest in the work of classical mathematical and geographical theoreticians like Strabo, Euclid and Claudius Ptolemy and the interest in following the course of the great discoveries initially exerted some influence on this development. The principal impulse, however, stemmed from practical necessity: of lawyers to understand issues that were in dispute; of antiquaries, clergymen and teachers to locate biblical events and historical episodes of classical and national antiquity; of an increasing number of merchants to plan and control their commercial activities and above all the requirements of the Henrician state from the late 1520s onwards for defence, administration and suitable display at court.

By the 1540s a wide variety of maps was being produced within England. This included maps of whole countries such as Palestine and Britain, regional maps, and large-scale maps and plans of towns, harbours, defence installations and military engagements, often of a pictorial nature. Foreign printed mapping was also being painted onto cloth for display as a cheap alternative to tapestry for royal and noble residences. The enthusiasm for maps among the ruling elite was comparable to the enthusiasm in our days for computers.

As late as the 1570s, however, the maps produced in England were almost exclusively manuscript. Italy, Germany and to a growing extent the Netherlands dominated the field of printed maps of all kinds because of their superior technology and organisation and because their geographical positions facilitated commercial distribution within Europe. Englishmen tended to purchase their maps and atlases from abroad and English mapmakers would send their work to the Netherlands to be engraved.

This was particularly true in the case of copperplate maps. These had been relatively common in Italy from the last quarter of the fifteenth century, but they only began to challenge the primacy of the woodcut north of the Alps from the 1520s. The earliest surviving detailed plan of London, the anonymous so-called 'Copperplate Plan', probably dating from the mid-1550s, of which only two plates and no contemporary impressions now survive, was probably engraved in the Netherlands[2] as were the county maps illustrating Speed's *Theatre of the Empire of Great Britain* in 1611.[3]

A few printed maps had, however, been published in England before Cole's map of Palestine of 1572. The first map to be printed in England was the woodcut map, possibly by Holbein, illustrating the Exodus that accompanied Coverdale's translation of the Bible and was printed in London in 1535.[4] Many more bible maps, illustrating the route of the Exodus, the Dream of Daniel, and the Holy Land and Eastern Mediterranean in general and based on the work of foreign cartographers were to follow.[5] Rough woodcut diagrams illustrating the Pinkie Clough campaign of 1547 had appeared in William Patten's *The Expedicion into Scotland* (London, 1548)[6] and these may be regarded as the earliest printed maps to be conceived by an Englishman and cut and printed in England. William Cuningham published a detailed woodcut map of Norwich to illustrate his *The Cosmographical Glasse* in 1559[7] and the Huguenot exile Giles Godet ('Godhede') is known to have published a series of small woodcut 'cards' of England and Scotland and other countries in 1562/3.[8] There were doubtless many more of such cheaply produced small woodcut maps that have not survived.

Close copies of existing copper plate maps had been engraved in London from the 1550s. The best-known example is the four-sheet map of Spain, the 'Nova descriptio Hispaniae', engraved and printed in England probably in 1553 by Thomas Gemini. This was a close copy of a map by Hieronymous Cock of 1553 which itself was closely modelled on a 1551 map of Spain by Vincenzo Paletino. No example of the first state, which appears to have been dedicated to Charles V, is now known, the sole recorded example being of the second state, dedicated to Philip II and Mary, and printed in 1555.[9]

A very few original maps had also been engraved on copper by Englishmen in England in this period. Almost certainly the printed world map by Sebastian Cabot of 1549 cut, apparently, by Clement Adams, the tutor of the royal pages, was a copperplate map.[10] Thirteen years later, in 1562, Adams supervised the production of a map of Muscovy, based on information from Anthony Jenkinson and William Borough. This map was engraved by Nicholas Reynolds, a Londoner, a correspondent of Ortelius and probably the same person who a decade later was to engrave one of Saxton's county maps. An example of the map of Muscovy which came to light in Wroclaw in 1988 is currently the earliest surviving copperplate map known to have been engraved as well as conceived by an Englishman.[11]

Cole's sole known cartographic work was in the tradition of Thomas Gemini. There is nothing original about it in terms of geographical content and it would seem that he was doing little more than advertising the engraving skills that he had acquired in the course of his work at the Mint and as an instrument maker. Such self-advertisement would have been timely in the early 1570s. Elizabeth I's leading minister, William Cecil, Lord Burghley, had for many years wished to see England and Wales mapped in detail for administrative purposes. By the early 1570s, probably encouraged by the utility of the maps in Ortelius's atlas he was clearly thinking in terms of printed maps of the counties of England.[12]

Because of his northern roots - acknowledged on his map of Palestine - Cole is likely to have been friendly with three of the mapmakers most closely associated with Lord Burghley's cartographic initiative: the Lancastrian Laurence Nowell (*c.* 1510-*c.* 1570), the Yorkshiremen John Rudd (1498-1579) and his pupil Christopher Saxton (*c.* 1542/4 - 1610/11).[13] Cole's map of Palestine could therefore have been an intentional bid on his part, based on his inside knowledge, to draw Burghley's attention to his engraving skills and to secure a commission to engrave some or all of the forthcoming county maps - or any other maps that might be produced officially or semi-officially in connection with the needs of government or of England's expansion overseas.

If indeed these were Cole's intentions, he was unsuccessful though he did succeed in winning other employment from Burghley. In the event, another North Country man, Augustine Ryther, was more successful. It was he who later in the 1570s engraved Saxton's county maps of Westmoreland, Cumberland, Durham and possibly Northumberland (1576), of Yorkshire and Gloucestershire (1577) and the introductory map of England and Wales (1579) as well, in later years, maps illustrating the course of the Armada of 1588 by Robert Adams, the son of Clement Adams, the gores for a celestial globe by Thomas Hood and a chart for Richard Hakluyt's *Principall Voyages*.[14]

There was a sharp increase in map engraving and publishing activity in London for about 20 years between the late 1570s and the mid-1590s. This was undertaken by leading protestant mapmakers and publishers from the southern Netherlands, notably Jodocus Hondius, who had found refuge in England and it ceased when they left for Amsterdam. A map engraving and printing industry of any size, only finally became established in England after 1660.[15]

Notes

1 For the next three paragraphs see most recently P.D.A. Harvey, *Maps in Tudor Britain* (London 1993); Peter Barber, 'England I: Pageantry Defense and Government: Maps at Court to 1550; England II: Monarchs, Ministers and Maps, 1550-1625', *Monarchs Ministers and Maps. The emergence of Cartography as a Tool of Government in Early Modern Europe*, ed. D. Buisseret (Chicago 1992), pp. 26 -98; P.M. Barber, 'Les Iles Britanniques', *Gerardi Mercatoris Atlas Europae*, ed. Marcel Watelet (Antwerp 1994), particularly pp. 43-5; P.M. Barber 'Cartography, Topography and History Painting', *The Inventories of Henry VIII*, ed. David Starkey (forthcoming).

2 James Howgego, *Printed Maps of London circa 1553-1850* (London 1978), pp. 8-9, 43 no.1. with bibliography; Felix Barker and Peter Jackson, *The History of London in Maps* (London 1990), pp. 14-15. Both surviving plates are now owned by the Museum of London.

3 R.A. Skelton, *County Atlases of the British Isles 1579-1850. A Bibliography. 1579-1703* (Folkestone 1970), pp. 33-4.

4 Catherine Delano Smith and Elizabeth Morley Ingram, *Maps in Bibles 1500-1600* (Geneva 1991), pp. 26-7, 144 (E 1535b); Elizabeth Morley Ingram, 'The Map of the Holy Land in the Coverdale Bible: a map by Holbein?' *The Map Collector* 64 (1993), pp. 21-31.

5 Delano Smith and Ingram, *op. cit., passim.*

6 Illustrated and discussed in J.R. Hale, *Artists and Warfare in the Renaissance* (New Haven and London 1990), pp.264-5

7 Reproduced in James Elliot, *The City in Maps. Urban mapping to 1900* (London 1987), pp. 40-1, pl. 20.

8 Edward Arber, *Transcript of the Stationers Registers* (London 1875), i, p.90.

9 Arthur H. Hind, *Engraving in England in the Sixteenth and Seventeenth Centuries. Part 1: The Tudor Period* (Cambridge 1952), pp 56-7; Robert Karrow, *Mapmakers of the Sixteenth Century and their Maps* (Chicago 1993), p. 252. In 1555 Gemini took impressions from the original plate, engraved in Italy, of George Lily's map of the British Isles which had originally appeared in Rome in 1546, altering only the imprint (Hind, pp. 57-8; Karrow, p. 253, Shirley, *Early Printed maps of the British Isles 1477-1650* (East Grinstead 1991), p. 28 no. 59).

10 Karrow, pp. 110-11. No example is now known. Karrow doubts whether Adams actually engraved the map, while Skelton felt that the map was a woodcut rather than an engraved copperplate. At all events the map is likely to

have been a modified version of Cabot's engraved world map of 1544 (for which see also Rodney Shirley, *The Mapping of the World. Early Printed World Maps 1472-1700* (London 1983), pp. 922-3, no. 81.)

[11] Karrow, pp. 318-320 and references cited there; Hind, p.99; Barber 1992, pp. 67, 74.

[12] See P.M. Barber, 'Les Iles Britanniques', art. cit. n. 1 above, particularly pp. 66-72; William Ravenhill, *Christopher Saxton's 16th Century Maps* (Shrewsbury 1992), pp. 9-20 and its brief but up-to-date bibliography.

[13] P.M. Barber, 'A Tudor Mystery: Laurence Nowell's Map of England and Ireland', *The Map Collector* 22 (March 1983), pp. 16-21; Barber 1994, pp. 68-70 and sources cited there for Nowell and Rudd; Ifor M. Evans and Heather Lawrence, *Christopher Saxton. Elizabethan Map-Maker* (Wakefield 1979).

[14] Evans and Lawrence, pp. 36, 39; Hind, pp. 138-149 who emphasises that, like Saxton, he came from the neighbourhood of Leeds.

[15] Sarah Tyacke, *London Map-Sellers 1660-1720* (Tring 1978); Sarah Tyacke, 'Map-Sellers and the London Map Trade *c.* 1650-1710', *My Head is a Map. A Festschrift for R.V. Tooley*, ed. H.M. Wallis and Sarah Tyacke (London 1973), pp. 63-80.

Humphrey Cole and the Frobisher Voyages

James McDermott

In the mid 1570s, two men - Martin Frobisher, a sometime privateer of Yorkshire antecedents and Michael Lok, mercer, merchant adventurer and member of a substantial London mercantile family - colluded to seek backing for a projected voyage to discover a north-western route to 'Cathay' and the entrepots of the Far East. In that immediate aim they succeeded: between 1576 and 1578, three voyages under the personal command of Frobisher sailed across the Atlantic Ocean to south-east Baffin Island (to the mariners, the landfall became known as *Meta Incognita*, the 'unknown limits'). These were the first European expeditions to the area for which a dependable record survives - that is, other than in a purely oral tradition, as is the case for the earlier Norse expeditions - yet an enterprise that was originally set out as a voyage of reconnaissance swiftly degenerated into an ill-considered speculation, when ore returned from a small island at the mouth of what is now Frobisher Bay was declared to contain quantities of gold and silver. The second (1577) voyage was devoted only to identifying and securing further ore deposits, whilst the final (1578) voyage consisted of 15 ships and 351 mariners, miners and soldiers; the largest expedition to the area prior to the present century. In Arctic weather conditions, these men mined and transported a total of almost 1,400 tons of ore which subsequently proved to be worthless; the enterprise, burdened with large debts and no income (other than from the already-worn pockets of its unfortunate investors), and increasingly mocked as a fool's venture, collapsed during the early part of 1579. If the episode bore any lessons for England's emerging maritime tradition, they were entirely negative.

Yet the project - in its original manifestation - drew to itself a significant proportion of England's existing expertise in a number of disciplines. The initiative of Lok and Frobisher was a reflection of a broader, economic imperative: at its most fundamental, to gain access to the potentially vast wealth of the trading routes established on the back of the great discoveries of the previous century; and more particularly, to exploit - in the name of England - a route to the 'new' markets of the East which lay sufficiently distant from the existing Spanish and Portuguese sea-lanes to avoid either unwelcome interest or outright hostility.

This was not a new goal. Since the 1550s, the Muscovy Company had been striving without success to find a north-eastern route via St Nicholas and Archangel. Its failure encouraged several of its own members - including Lok, the Company's London Agent - to seek alternatives which theoretically contravened the Company's patent rights to seek and exploit such discoveries. Though Lok took the lead in this, he quickly secured the financial support of a Governor of the Company, Sir Lionel Ducket; one of the original charter-members, Alderman William Bonde; the former Company ambassador to the Russian Court, Thomas Randolphe; and the outstanding early Anglo-Russian trader, Anthony Jenkinson. For his part, Martin Frobisher - probably with the assistance of his sponsor, the Earl of Warwick - secured investments from several members of the Queen's Privy Council, including the Earls of Leicester, Sussex and Warwick himself, Francis Walsingham and the Lord Treasurer, Burghley.

The venture therefore claimed the early support of substantial figures in both Court and City. Though under-financed (almost half the required funds were loaned from Lok's own pocket), the adventurers clearly attempted to provide a high standard of equipment and intelligence to enable the reconnaissance to succeed. A small bark - the *Michael*, of 20-25 tons burden - was purchased, and a new bark, *Gabriel*, built for the voyage by one of England's leading shipwrights, Matthew Baker.[1] Technical assistance was obtained from William Borough, one of the leading Muscovy Company navigators, and John Dee, England's foremost theoretical mathematician and hydrographer. These men probably assisted Lok (whose own knowledge of cosmography and related disciplines was substantial) to purchase texts, charts and instruments of navigation for the forthcoming voyage. As treasurer of the enterprise, Lok kept the account books, all of which - uniquely - have survived. These reveal, in minute detail, how the adventurers' precious funds were expended; and it is here that we find the first evidence of Humphrey Cole's involvement with the project:

'theis Instrumentes to be restored.

paid for divers Instrumentes for Navigation as followithe.
for ii paper bookes for Accomptes li o. 9. o

paid for a booke of Cosmografie in frenche of
Andreas Thevet makinge li 2. 4. o

paid to Humfrye Cole and others, as followithe
for a great globe of metall in blanke in a
case of leather li 7. 13. 4
for a great Instrument of brasse named *Armilla Tolomei*, or hemispherium, with a case li 4. 6. 8
paid for an Instrument of brasse named *Sphera Nautica* with a case li 4. 6. 8
for a great Instrument of brasse named *Compassum Meridianum*, with a case li 4. 6. 8
for a great Instrument of brase named *Holometrum Geometricum*, with a case li 4. o. o
for a great Instrument of brase named *Horologium Universale*, with a case li 2. 6. 8
for a ring of brase named *Annalus Astronomicus* li 1. 10. o
for a litell standinge levell of brase li o. 6. 8
for a case with smalle instrumentes for geometrie, of yron li o. 6. 8
for an Instrument of wood, a stafe named *Balistella*, with a case li o. 13. 4
for a verye great Carte of Navigacon li 5. o. o
for a greate mappe universall of Mercator in prente li 1. 6. 8
for iii other small mapps prented li o. 6. 8
for vi Cartes of navigacon written in blanke parchment wherof 4 ruled playne and 2 rounde li 2. o. o
for a bible englishe, great volume li 1. o. o
for a Cosmografical glasse & castell knowlege li o. 10. o
for a newe world of Andreas Thevett englishe and frenche bookes ii smalle li o. 6. 8
for a regiment of Medina, spanishe li o. 3. 4
for Sir John Mandevylle, englishe li o. 1. o
for a Carte of Ortelius, prynte li (blank)
paid to William Thomas compasse maker for 20 Compasses of divers sortes li 3. 3. o
for 18 hower glasses li o. 17. o
some paid him li 4. o. o
paid for an Astrolabium, of William Burowe li 3. 10. o

some paid for Instrumentes li 50. 14. o[2]

It is likely that most, if not all, the major instruments were supplied by Cole himself. He may also have supplied - though not fashioned - the two metal spheres, possibly of 14-20 inches in diameter, for use at sea. The 'great globe of metall in blanke' was probably a terrestrial globe without land markings, to enable the prospective mariners to learn how to lay a course which was not distorted by the limitations of the plane chart.[3] The 'Armilla Tolomaei' or armillary sphere, was a celestial globe, possibly a companion sphere to the above-mentioned terrestrial globe, upon which the plotting of constellations would be effected. The 'Sphera Nautica' presents some problems; it is not clear whether this was a globe with rhumb (direction) lines engraved upon it, or a device for finding the variation between true and magnetic North. Clearly, however, the 'Compassum Meridianum' was acquired to establish variation, and the 'Holometrum Geometrum' - a precursor of the theodolite - was a bearing plate mounted upon an open sight with adjustments for bearings and elevation, used to chart unknown coastlines. The 'Horologium Universale' and 'Annalus Astronomicus' represented a degree of duplication; respectively, these were a universal dial and an astronomical ring; both were designed to establish time by the sun's altitude at a particular latitude, albeit employing slightly different methods.[4]

An astrolabe - to take the sun's altitude - was also purchased, not from Cole, but from William Borough. It is not clear whether this was a universal planispheric (or 'land' astrolabe, perhaps purchased for the tuition of Frobisher and his ships' masters) or a mariner's ring for use at sea, although subsequent comments regarding the difficulty of employing an astrolabe above 60° North indicates that an example of the latter instrument was certainly taken on the voyage.[5] Finally, the 'litell standinge levell of brase' supplied by Cole was probably filled with water to provide accurate levelling.

The expedition did not - could not - fulfil its stated aim of discovering a northwest route to the Far East. However, upon its return to England, Frobisher expressed his conviction that the 'strait' he had discovered was the true passage, and plans were drawn up for a further voyage. New investors came forward and set down their provisional subscriptions, even prior to the surprise announcement that a piece of ore returned from the New World contained significant proportions of gold. In the meantime, Humphrey Cole was employed in repairing the ships' instruments, whose buffeting in North Atlantic storms must have been severe. An entry in Lok's accounts show that he was paid £7. 11s. for this and for supplying certain new, unspecified instruments.[6] However, learning from the experience, the adventurers also hired a 'soldiare Instrument maker' named Anthony Rambridge, to accompany the forthcoming second voyage. Rambridge's dual occupation is an interesting reminder of the way in which England's developing military needs fostered the growth of a domestic industry in the production of scientific instruments, yet the rate of pay set down for the estimable gentleman does not suggest that his peculiar skills commanded much of a premium.[7]

Cole's involvement in supplying the enterprise with its instruments of navigation is hardly surprising, given his pre-eminence among contemporary domestic instrument makers. However, he was also to become associated with the assayers whose efforts to wrest some evidence of value from the New World ore began in the early months of 1577 and continued, with scant success, until the collapse of the enterprise two years later. Yet a brief examination of his career and contacts make this latter involvement seem equally logical. In his capacity both as a maker of precision instruments and an officer of the Royal Mint, Cole must have required a detailed understanding of all stages in the process of metal refining. He must also have been well-known to another officer of the Tower, the Master of Ordnance, Sir William Winter, whose dealings in respect of an early sample of ore returned from Frobisher's first voyage make him one of the two chief suspects (the other being Michael Lok himself) in promoting the subsequent gold-fever.[8] Cole may have been involved in Winter's early proofs of the ore, though there is no firm evidence of this. Once the existence of the ore became public knowledge on or around the 31 March 1577, the adventurers succumbed to the contemporary prejudice that German assayers were more adept than their English counterparts, and the sole right to work the ore was eventually to be disputed between Jonas Schutz, a Saxon working in Keswick with the Company of Mines Royal, and Burchard Kranich, who had treated the Queen in his capacity as a physician and had formerly been involved in the Cornish silver and lead refining trades.

Nevertheless, Englishmen continued to assist in the process. The second voyage returned from Baffin Island with almost 160 tons of ore, this time of several varieties found at various sites in and around an inlet on the northern shore of Frobisher Bay, named (and which remains) the Countess of Warwick's Sound, in honour of the wife of one of Frobisher's most enthusiastic Court backers. Proofs began almost immediately upon this new supply of ore. In the process of attempting to secure their own, exclusive rights to work it, Schutz and Kranich consistently 'discovered' some value in successive trials, though the precise results were anything but consistent. This optimistic ambiguity, coupled with the undoubted difficulties of refining ore of a type unfamiliar to any European assayer, undoubtedly prevented a rational assessment of its true value. On the 8 March 1578, Humphrey Cole attended an assay at Muscovy House, where a small furnace had been constructed following the collapse of that at Sir William Winter's 'house' (probably a small shed constructed in the grounds of Winter's warehouse at Tower Hill). This latest assay was conducted by Schutz and certified by Cole and two English assayers; it was proclaimed to have yielded gold and silver to the value of £23. 15s. per ton.[9] As it was the results of this assay that was to form the basis of recommendations to the Privy Council that a third voyage should be despatched (one whose scale was to burst the bubble of speculation in the project), it seems that Humphrey Cole had an indirect influence upon the ultimate fate of the enterprise. Like every other Englishman in attendance, Cole probably allowed himself to be convinced by what he was told he had seen, and certified the results without comment.

As the months passed without definitive results, and the third voyage dispatched and then returned with over a thousand tons of ore, the pressure upon the assayers to justify their efforts increased (the adventurers had yet to be furnished with the smallest piece of gold or silver from successive assays). By this time, Frobisher and Lok had become enemies, each blaming the other for the increasing financial pressures upon the enterprise. Prior to the despatch of the third voyage, Lok had championed the claims of Schutz against Kranich, and Frobisher those of the latter; both assayers were assiduous in blaming anything but their own skills for the poor results of their labours. Kranich was ultimately to fall from contention, being in very poor health and having been discovered adding silver-bearing antimonies to his proofs; but even with his role now unchallenged, Schutz found it impossible to derive any substantive value from his assays upon the ore.[10] He blamed the size of the refining facilities (at which large new works were planned and hurriedly built at Bignours mill, outside Dartford, Kent), and the quality of the 'additaments' he used in the refining process.[11] It was on this last matter that Humphrey Cole once more bestowed the benefit of his expertise.

An account of the various assays carried out in 1577-8,[12] written by one of Schutz's supporters (possibly at the behest of, but not by, Michael Lok), reveals that Schutz wanted a certain type of 'marquesite' (possibly pyrite) to use in the smelt; something that he suggested might be sought by

'Denham (Robert Denham, one of the English assayers assisting) or Coole'. This was on the 28 January 1578. On that recommendation, the Privy Council authorized - or ordered - Humphrey Cole to find the required additament. Cole concurred, and though it is not clear whether he began his search immediately or after a pause of some months, he eventually went where any sensible fellow might seek the right sort of coal - Newcastle. Michael Lok's accounts for the building works at Dartford contain entries dated 24 September 1578: 'paid mark Rowe pursar of the bark rowe for fraight of 14 tonnes of Cole m(ar)quesite sent by humphry Cole from newcastell at vi^{s} viii^{d} tonne and for prymage and Loadmenage to the mynerall(e)s 7^{sh} - li 5. 0. 0.'; 6 November: 'paid to Umphrye Cole for chardg(e)s of the m(ar)quesyt w(hi)ch came from newe Castell - li 4. 0. 0.' and 12 November: 'paid for lighterage of 16 tonne Secole marquesyte to dartforde'.[13] Cole had already been rewarded for his efforts; indeed, in view of the increasingly parlous state of the finances of the 'Company of Cathay', he seems to have exercised considerable prudence in insisting upon cash up-front. Lok's accounts for the 3 January 1579 note: 'paid to humphry Cole, in Jullie last for his chardges to newcastell for Secole marksyt for Workes at dartford, summ - li 20. 0. 0.'[14]

All the expertise of Cole in the fashioning of instruments and selection of refining additives was to little avail. Almost £25,000 had been expended by the adventurers, the majority of it on no greater evidence of the presence of gold in the New World ore than the testimony of assayers whose actual skills were eclipsed by their reputations. In the early months of 1579 the enterprise collapsed, and the adventurers crept away to nurse wounds of various size in their purses. At the end of the previous year, Michael Lok had made an offer to work the ore at Dartford for a period of three years at his own charge in return for unstated recompense; however, the offer was conditional upon a *quietus est* on bonds for £4,000 he had deposited in the Exchequer as surety for the Queen's investment in the enterprise, so we may assume that his offer was but a screen for the more urgent matter (Lok was to go to debtor's prison upon at least eight occasions between 1580-1, for outstanding debts of freight charges incurred in his name on behalf of his fellow adventurers). At the foot of this document, Humphrey Cole was named as being one of the 'workmen' on the ore.[15] As for the ore itself, Camden reported that it was eventually cast out to mend the local roads around Dartford.[16] A portion of wall, containing many pieces of a black composite ore alien to Europe, may still be seen upon application to the Curator of the Dartford Borough Museum, Mr Peter Boreham.

Notes

1 Public Record Office, Exchequer King's Remembrancer, E164/35 (hereafter PRO EKR E164/35), p. 9.

The cost of the *Gabriel*, with a 7 ton pinnace, decks and masts, was £105. 16s. 8d.

2 Ibid, pp. 16-17.

3 Contemporary cartographers did not know how to accurately represent meridians of longitude upon a chart. These were usually depicted in parallel, which meant that any ship's course laid upon the chart as a straight line would result in the vessel sailing increasingly south-west of its intended course as it passed through successive meridians. The use of a globe would prevent this, as meridians of longitude would be depicted as properly converging towards the Poles thereon. The globe purchased by Lok for the forthcoming voyage was by far the single most expensive aid to navigation he acquired; at £7. 13. 4. more than double the cost of the astrolabe.

4 The above analysis of ship's instruments is taken from J. McDermott and D.W. Waters, *Cathay and the way thither: The Navigation of the Frobisher voyages*; Canadian Museum of Civilization, Meta Incognita Project, 1997; (unpublished) ARTAF Research Report no. 16, pp. 12-13; and D.W. Waters, *The Art of Navigation in England in Elizabethan and early Stuart Times* (London 1958); appendix 10c, pp. 531-2.

5 George Best, *A True Discourse of the Late Voyages of Discoverie for finding of a Passage to Cathaya by the North-Weast, under the Conduct of Martin Frobisher General* (London 1578), *The Three Voyages of Martin Frobisher*, ed. R. Collinson (Hakluyt Society, London 1867), p. 155: 'And here (ie. at *c.* 61 degrees north) the north starre is so muche elevated above the horizon, that with the staffe it is hardly to be wel observed, and the degrees in the Astrolabe are too small to observe minutes. Therefore we alwaies used the staffe and the sunne, as fittest instruments for this use'.

6 PRO EKR E164/35, p. 102.

7 Ibid, p. 142. Rambridge received wages of £5. 11. 1. at the return of the second voyage, while the basic rate of soldier's pay was £5. Their sergeant, Edmund English, received £7. 6. 8. It is possible that Rambridge was employed chiefly to service the assay balances taken on the voyage by Jonas Schutz (who was to test samples of ore on-site); certainly, there was a limit to the repairs that could be carried out upon complex scientific instruments at sea, or in the harsh, ill-provided climate of Baffin Island.

8 SP 12/112/25, 'Mr Lockes Discoors touching the Ewre, 1577'. Lok, relating his own, secret efforts to have a piece of the ore assayed by an Italian assayer, Giovanni Baptista Agnello, claimed that Winter had admitted to him that he, Sir John Barkeley, Sir William Morgan and others had made proofs of another piece at 'a howsse at Lambethe' and also at Winter's own house at Tower Hill. This was at

a time (late March, 1577) before the existence of ore, let alone its supposed value, had been disclosed publicly.

[9] SP 12/123/7.

[10] Like his rival Kranich, Schutz seems to have deliberately 'salted' his assays with precious metals. The Queen's auditors' report on Michael Lok's account books, dated 6 May 1581, stated that: ' ... thomas allyn (Allen replaced the discredited Lok as 'treasurer' of the company of adventurers in December 1578; his only role was to attempt to secure outstanding subscriptions and raise funds from the sale of equipment to pay off outstanding debts) Receued of Michael Lok, two Ingott(e)s of fyne gold, weinge ix penyweight & viii graines / and two Ingot(e)s of fine syluer, weinge vii onces, xviii penyweight & xii graines / w(hi)ch said gold & syluer proceded of the meltinge of the Ewer brought from META INCOGNITA in the second voiage, by the workmanship of Jonas shutz ...' (PRO EKR E164/36, p. 332).

[11] 'Additaments' was the contemporary terminology for the various additives which allowed the separation of gold or silver bearing lead from the slag during the smelting process. On contemporary refining techniques, see D.D. Hogarth, P.W. Boreham and J.G. Mitchell, *Mines, Minerals, Metallurgy*, Canadian Museum of Civilization, Mercury Series, Directorate paper 7 (1994), Appendix 1.

[12] 'A Little bundle of the tryeing of ye Northwest Ewre, by Dr Burcot, Jonas Schutz, Baptista Agnillo, etc': SP 12/122/62.

[13] Entries contained in PRO EKR E164/36, pp. 181-3.

[14] Ibid, p. 186.

[15] British Library, Lansdowne MS 30/4, f.12

[16] William Camden, *The History of the most renowned and victorious princess Elizabeth, late Queen of England* (London 1675), p. 216.

Humphrey Cole at the Mint

B.J. Cook

Humphrey Cole was active at the Tower mint for around 15 years in the post of die-sinker, or sinker of irons, a post also sometimes known as the under-graver. Neither the exact dates, nor the precise circumstances of either his appointment or departure are known. By his own account, in 1578, he had been at the mint for 20 years (Gunther 1927: 311), but in fact he does not appear before 1563 as the established successor to John Lawrence, who had become die-sinker in 1545 (Challis 1975: 58 and 63). Lawrence's contract obliged him 'to instruct his successor' (Craig 1953: 121). However, Cole may not have needed much in the way of training, as his background was probably as a goldsmith, as he so described himself on the cartouche on his map of the Holy Land of 1272 (Gunther 1927: 305). This would, indeed, be the normal background for a mint worker of his type (Challis 1978: 34-5).

By 1576 there was a second sinker of irons working alongside Cole, and presumably being instructed in his turn. This was George Tyson, who had been employed at the mint as a labourer from 1560 at a salary of £10 p.a (Challis 1975: 69-70). Cole's latest recorded involvement with the mint was in 1578 (Challis 1975: 58). Tyson remained as sinker after Cole's departure until 1603, apparently working alone until 1596, when John Rutlinger became under-engraver alongside him (Challis 1975: 67).

The sinker of irons was one of a small group of mint operatives whose task was the production of the dies with which the coinage would be struck. In the 1560s most of them were direct crown employees, in line with the system of mint organisation introduced to cope with Henry VIII's debasement policies in 1544. Under this system mint workers were salaried employees of the crown. In 1572 the older system of contracting out the mint operations to an individual known as the mint-master or master-worker was restored, with, in theory, only a few supervisory posts remaining directly paid by the crown: the warden, assay-master, porter and clerk of the irons. These were all posts with considerable security responsibilities, and their incumbents were the crown's main safeguard against fraud within the mint. However, the existing holders of the other posts (including the sinker of irons) remained in place under the new regime, and in practice when they left they were replaced much as before. They were, however, paid by the mint-master, not by the crown (Challis 1975: 52).

Under the overall authority of the mint warden, the chief of the officials concerned with the dies was the engraver (sometimes called chief engraver), with a salary of £30 a year. In the early sixteenth century this post had been held as a court sinecure by the likes of courtiers such as Henry Norris, who employed skilled deputies to do the actual work (Challis 1978: 30). Following the mint reorganisation of 1544 this changed, with the current deputy Henry Basse becoming engraver in his own right at £20 p.a., raised to £30 in 1545 (Challis 1975: 55). From 1551 until his death in 1596 the post of engraver was held by Derek Anthony, latterly assisted and then succeeded by his son Charles Anthony (Challis 1975: 54; see also Symonds 1913: 358-60).

The engraver's job, as described in 1560, was 'to engrave puncheons and in time of need to sink dies' (Craig 1953: 121). His job, therefore, was to produce the main punches (above all the portrait punches) which would then be used to make the working dies. The engraver may also have been responsible for a master portrait, perhaps in the form of a drawing or painting. It is certainly known that the queen gave a sitting to Eloy Mestrell at Richmond in 1560 when he was preparing his experimental mechanised coinage (Challis 1978: 18), and it is highly likely that Derek Anthony made similar preparations for the regular coinage. Later, in the 1580s, the 'graver of the irons' accompanied two painters in an expedition to court 'concerning the drawing of the stamped money' (Symonds 1916: 89). Recent work on the coin portraits of Elizabeth I has demonstrated that numbers of portrait punches prepared at the same time share enough stylistic elements to indicate such a common source (Brown and Comber 1988: 90-1).

The sinker of irons ranked second in this group of officers. In 1553 John Lawrence's salary in the post was raised from £10 to £20 p.a., and Tyson's salary as sinker was also £20 p.a. This was Cole's salary throughout his tenure, a level he later claimed to be 'lacking sufficiente maintenance for me and my family', though it was on top of lodgings and another £3 p.a. 'diett' allowance (Gunther 1927: 310-11); he may have had a point, given the price inflation of the late sixteenth century. Safeguarding the completed dies was an administrator, the clerk of the irons, on a salary of £13 6s.8d. a year. There were two incumbents during Cole's time at the mint: Humphrey Welles, in post from 1557 to 1569, and Robert Horneby, from 1569 to 1583 (Challis 1975: 70 and 61-2). Then there was the mint smith, whose job would have been to prepare the iron to make the dies, and cast it into the necessary shape. William Hopkins, a blacksmith of London, held the post from at least 1560 until 1596 on a salary of £10 p.a (Challis 1975: 61). In the 1570s he incurred the displeasure of the mint warden Richard Martin for his private work in producing 'calivers and great iron pieces', and for stripping lead from mint buildings (Challis 1992: 256).

The core job of the die sinker was to create the working dies by punching the design of the coin into the face of the prepared die. His tools would be the fairly elaborate punches provided by the engraver for the main design elements, above all the royal portrait, and the alternative images on some of the gold coins such as the angel, with its complicated design of the Archangel Michael fighting the dragon. Other punches would be for the less elaborate design features, such as the lions and fleurs-de-lis in the reverse shield, and for initial marks and the rose behind the queen's bust on several of the silver denominations. He would also use a series of fonts of letter punches for the different coin denominations, ranging from the large 30-shilling sovereign down to the tiny three-farthings (the smallest coin of the reign to carry a legend). Also, some of the silver denominations had the year of issue prominently on the reverse, just above the shield.

The sinker may also have been responsible for finishing the die, by hardening the die-face to prepare it for striking, although this job could have been passed on to the smith. It has to be said that the division of labour here described is assumed from the job title, and it is certainly conceivable that, depending on ability and need, the sinker of irons might help make the coin punches, and also that the smith or other mint employee helped make up the dies. A rule proposed later in the reign allowed for either the engraver or sinker to be involved in adding certain features to the die (Symonds 1913: 359), and it may be significant that Cole's successor as sinker moved up from being a mint labourer.

Recent research by Brown and Comber (1988) provides some insights into the provision and use of punches in the Elizabethan mint. The dies for the portrait punches which had been developed during the 1561 recoinage (Brown and Comber's bust 3) were still available to the die-sinker throughout the 1560s and 70s, although they were joined by new ones in 1566 (bust 4), 1573 (bust 5) and 1583 (bust 6), which were used alongside them for some denominations. A single portrait punch might thus be useable for 10 to 15 years, and make hundreds of dies. Brown and Comber have identified nine shilling-sized portrait punches from the period of the 1561 recoinage, along with 10 for the smaller denominations.

As shillings were not in production during Cole's tenure as sinker, it was the latter that he was using mostly, although the shilling-sized bust was also employed on the gold half-pound, in production until 1572. A second version of bust 3 was used also on the gold half-pound, but its main employment would have been on the sixpence. A third size was for the gold half-crown, and silver threepence and half-groat; a fourth for the three-halfpence; and a fifth for the penny and three-farthings. When bust 4 was introduced in 1566, four different sizes were provided: for the gold half-pound; the silver sixpence; the gold crown; and one for the gold half-crown, and silver threepence and half-groat. Portrait punches using bust 5 were confined to two, one for the sixpence and another for the penny and three-farthings (Brown and Comber 1988: 93-4). (See Figure 46 for illustrations of some of these coins.)

When Cole came to the mint it had recently concluded probably its greatest achievement of the sixteenth century: the recall of the debased coinage current since Henry VIII began the Great Debasement in 1544, and its replacement with a fine silver coinage of the old sterling standard (Challis 1978: 119-28). The bulk of this task was achieved between September 1560 and October 1561, with £742,233's worth of silver coin produced between December 1560 and October 1561, and another £194,440 in November 1561-November 1562. 1561-2 also saw the reign's most significant output of gold coin, £75,133's worth, replacing the gold of the debasement period (Challis 1992: 686-7). The recoinage was regarded by Elizabeth herself, and by subsequent historians, as one of the great achievements of her reign: in his *Annals* Camden said it 'turned to her greater, yea greatest glory'. The queen made a formal visit to the mint in July 1561 to congratulate her staff (Challis 1978: 127). An issue of medals commemorated the recoinage, bearing the legend BENE CONSTITUTA RE NUMMARIA (Hawkins 1885: 99-100).

A document of mint expenditure in 1560 records the production costs of 192 dozen of piles and trussels (upper and lower dies) for shillings, groats, half-groats and pence, and 'gold irons' (dies for the gold coinage), that is, 2,304 dies in all. Further payments were made for another 146 dozen, giving 4,056 dies certainly produced in that year (Symonds 1916: 67). It is not impossible that these were all the dies needed for the recoinage. Estimating the likely output of dies is a risky and controversial business, but it is recorded that dies for fourteenth-century silver pennies (about the size of the Elizabethan half-groat) might strike 20,000 coins per pair of dies, so 2,000 pairs of dies could be responsible for on the order of 40 million coins (see, for instance, Stewart 1964). The 1560-1 recoinage may have been responsible for something around 50 million coins (and possibly rather fewer), so (allowing for a great many assumptions) the match of known numbers of dies to known output is of the right order of magnitude.

Cole's arrival was in the immediate aftermath of this huge effort, the dies for which were provided by his predecessor, John Lawrence together with an assistant William Cure (Challis 1975: 58; Symonds 1913: 359) and inevitably the demands placed on him were much smaller. As usual for the mint at this time, its records of output give the total amount of metal coined, but not the weight of metal used for each particular denomination. During Cole's 15-year tenure, £1,108,509's worth of silver was coined, an average of £73,900 a year; plus £210,777's worth in gold, a yearly average of £14,052 (Challis 1992: 686-7). Of course, mint output fluctuated from year to year, along with the quantity of bullion submitted for coining.

In these years 12 denominations were in production (though not necessarily consistently so): in gold, the half-pound, crown and half-crown up till 1572, and thereafter the angel, half-angel, and quarter-angel; and in silver the sixpence, threepence, half-groat, three-halfpence, penny and three-farthings (see Figure 46). So if, for example, during Cole's tenure all of an average year's silver was turned into the largest current denomination (i.e. sixpences), the output of numbers of coins would have been around 3 million (the recoinage year of 1560-1 would have generated nearly 30 million sixpences).

A sixteenth-century die was probably expected to make several thousand (perhaps as many as 10-20,000) strikings during its working life. Thus, with a coinage output of the level known for Cole's tenure, the demand for new dies each year was probably of the order of a few hundred. The die-sinker would be expected to ensure that there was available a stock of usable dies at all times, presumably in consultation with the clerk of the irons. It has been suggested that this consisted of sufficient dies to cover a month's coining (Brown 1958: 570). It seems clear that Cole's workload as sinker left him with plenty of time for other projects (his earliest dated instrument is from 1568: Gunther 1927: 281).

Periodically the standards of the English coinage were checked in the trial of the pyx, and under Elizabeth coinage produced between each pyx trial had a distinct mark, known as the initial mark or privy mark: a small symbol or shape, such as a rose, coronet, acorn or crescent, standing at the head of the coin's legend on both sides. It was this which defined the issue. On some denominations (the sixpence, threepence, three-halfpence and three-farthings), the date was also present on the coin's reverse. A third design feature with security implications was the rose which appeared behind the queen's head on alternate silver denominations: sixpence, threepence, threehalfpence and threefarthings, but not on the shilling, groat, half-groat and penny. This helped tell the denominations apart.

The need to maintain a stock of dies was sometimes made problematic by the occurrence of a pyx trial, which changed the valid initial mark, and also by shifts in output levels. Simply disposing of inaccurate dies was wasteful (in 1599 the mint-master complained bitterly when the mint-warden introduced such a policy, of having serviceable dies scrapped instead of overstamped (Craig 1953: 129)). Humphrey Cole was faced with a number of these situations. Indeed, he may have been presented with such a problem very soon after his arrival. In 1563 there was a large stock of dies dated 1562 still remaining, presumably left over from a level of die production designed for the 1561 recoinage. However, by 1563 mint output had, inevitably, fallen sharply. The 1562 dies were overstamped, presumably by Cole, with later dates, being changed to both 1563 and 1564 (Brown 1958: 571; see also below Figure 46 nos 7-8). (The survival of these dies into 1564 was facilitated by the arrival of plague in London in the summer of 1563: the mint was closed down through autumn and winter.)

One way to stop these problems recurring was to leave the initial mark off the newly-made die at first, only adding it when the die was being brought into use, and/or similarly omitting the last digit of the date. The dating of coins had itself only begun in 1549, and it appears that the problem had already been faced in Mary Tudor's mint, as at least one die for the dated shillings reads just 155-, with the last digit omitted in error (Carlyon-Britton 1953: 325).

Nevertheless, it does not seem that Cole revived this practice for dates. In 1568 he still needed to overstamp sixpences originally dated 1567 (Brown 1958: 572), a similar situation ocurred in 1577-8 (Figure 46, no. 11), and on other occasions the incorrect date was allowed to stand with a correct initial mark. For example, three-halfpence of initial mark acorn exist dated 1572, although the mark was only in use from November 1573, and other incorrectly dated coins are known for initial marks castle (1570-2), ermine (1572-4) and eglantine (1574-8) (Brown 1958: 570; and see, for example, below Figure 46, nos 10 and 13). The mint was fairly tolerant of inaccurate dates, since it was the initial mark which defined the issue.

However, it was therefore essential for the initial mark to be correctly indicated. Mint practice under Cole was not consistent. Coins survive with the initial mark castle (1570-2) overstamped on initial mark coronet (1567-70) (Figure 46, no. 10). However, sometimes the initial mark may have been left off new dies until actual use, since on at least one die, used for the 1574 threepence, this was mistakenly omitted altogether (Brown 1958: 571). Also, on some coins dated 1572, where the initial mark combines with the 'wrong' date (Figure 46, no. 13), there had clearly been no overstamping, so, again, the space for the initial mark must have been left vacant until the die was needed (Brown 1958: 572). Yet, other coins from the same issue (dated 1572, but with later initial marks) have one mark stamped over another e.g. eglantine (1574-8) over ermine (1572-3) (Brown 1958: 272).

Cole's dies rarely omitted the rose behind the queen's head, but this slip does occur on at least one die, a threepence of 1568 (Figure 46, no. 12). Similarly there are a couple of occurrences of missing dates on the backs of sixpences (Brown 1958: 573; see, for instance, Figure 46, no. 9). Mis-spellings in the legends rarely occur. Overall, the standards of die production under Humphrey Cole were generally high, give or take the odd such slip-up. The problems arising from the need to correct dates or initial marks were of a different nature. They represented not mistakes in manufacture, but in the estimating of demand. When this occurred Cole's solution does not appear always consistent.

It must be said that, from the surviving coins, these situations do not seem to have been particularly common under Cole, and it may be that he and/or his colleagues were generally fairly successful in estimating the numbers of dies required in normal circumstances, or that, in most cases, there was a fairly consistent practice of leaving the place for at least the initial mark empty until late in the day. The few examples of overstamped marks may each be the result of particular circumstances: the initial mark added to just a few left-over dies. It was even possible for dies to be altered once they had begun striking. There are certainly late-medieval examples of this, and it would have been a shame to waste a perfectly good die in the early stages of its working life (for an example, see Cook 1991: 195 no. 81). After all, all that really mattered was that coinage with the correct initial mark was being produced.

It may be that Cole was not always the only one involved in die-sinking, and that the imput of colleagues or assistants was responsible for any apparent lack of consistency. When the same problems recurred significantly later in the reign, it was threatened that if the engraver or sinker negligently omitted the privy mark or the rose from any punch, even if only two or three pieces were struck, the mint-master should be fined the enormous sum of £2,000 (Symonds 1913: 359). Not surprisingly this proposal aroused great resistance from the mint-master and it was was not put into effect. In 1560 the engraver's job had been described as including die sinking in time of need, an obvious requirement with the recoinage impending (Craig 1953: 121), and in 1572 the new mint organisation included the provision that the posts of graver and sinker be united after Derek Anthony's death, a proposal never in fact carried out (Gunther 1927: 310). As reflections of possible mint practice these cases suggest the possibility of some overlap in the activities of the engraver and sinker. However, there is no obvious occasion during Cole's tenure to require such extra effort, though he was certainly using assistance by the 1570s (see below).

It was during the 1560s that the mint saw England's first experiments with mechanised coining techniques (Borden and Brown 1983). Eloy Mestrell was presumably responsible for making his own dies, and he was certainly given a sitting by the queen for the master portrait, from which he made his portrait punches (Challis 1989: 257). His machinery was not found to be as efficient as the current hammered method, but he was permitted to produce modest amounts of coin, mostly sixpences, at various times during the decade. Whether he made all his own dies, or whether the other mint officers had a hand is not clear. The milled coinage dies had a distinct manufacturing technique, with substantial re-engraving of the die-face, once the basic design had been applied with punches in the usual way (Borden and Brown 1983: 112).

Mestrell would presumably have had some co-operation with Cole over access to tools and materials. This may have been curtailed after a brush with the law over counterfeiting in 1568-9. When Mestrell resumed his activities in 1570, he had only limited access to letter punches: the only set made available to him had a retrograde N, which may suggest he had always been, or had become dependent on the die-workshop for his letter punches (Borden and Brown 1983: 110; see below Figure 46, no. 19). A medallion of the queen he produced at the same time had the reverse design of the Tower (site of the mint) with the legend QUID HOC SINE ARMES (What is this without tools?), which could be interpreted as a complaint of his current lack of access to die-making equipment (Borden and Brown 1983: 110-11). When Richard Martin became mint-warden in 1572, he was determined to be rid of Mestrell, and the expenses he entailed. One of the costs he laid against him was for taking ironwork from the smith of the mint worth £30, perhaps for making dies or punches (Goldman 1974: 425).

That Cole may have had a fairly close working relationship to Mestrell is suggested by his petition to Lord Burghley in 1578 (Gunther 1927: 311). He describes his appointment as being owed directly to Burghley, and his job as being 'to doe the servyces perteyninge to the mill', with the promise of the reversion of Mestrell's post and perquisites on the latter's death or removal. His post as die-sinker (which he had by then held for well over 15 years) he describes as being in effect a temporary position, until Mestrell's post became vacant: possibly a disingenuous claim. The occasion of this letter was in the aftermath Mestrell's execution on charges of counterfeiting in the spring of 1578. While he had not produced any coinage since about 1572, his machinery had remained and was used by someone (perhaps Derek Anthony, perhaps, given his professed interest, Humphrey Cole) to produce a group of patterns in 1574-5, and he had kept his Tower lodgings (Borden and Brown 1983: 111).

This petition of Cole to Burghley for Mestrell's 'house, office and ffee', dated December 1578, seems to mark the end of his mint career. Perhaps the rejection of his petition was a significant factor. In it he claims that half of his annual salary of £20 was currently paying for 'he that nowe exerciseth that place', i.e. as sinker of the dies, who 'nowe...refuseth to serve in it anie longer'. This was presumably George Tyson, the mint labourer paid £10 p.a., who would succeed Cole, and who was in post as a die-sinker from about 1576. The implication is that Tyson had in practice been doing all the mint-work of the die-sinker, while Cole had been pursuing his other activities. Tyson may have been unwilling to see this situation continue, and Cole was unwilling to reassume his former duties. Perhaps in seeking to replace Mestrell, he hoped to retain mint lodgings and perhaps an increased salary (Mestrell had had an annuity of £25) in a post which involved virtually no work.

Cole's final time at the mint was during a period of some disruption caused by a long and bitter conflict between the warden, Richard Martin, watchdog of standards, and the mint-master, John Lonyson, who organised the coinage production and, Martin believed, was deliberately manufacturing coin below the prescribed standards. The conflict came to a compromise solution in 1578, and both Lonyson and Martin remained in post (Challis 1992: 256-7). The strong-minded Martin had always been hostile to Mestrell, and the pointless expense he entailed. He is unlikely to have accepted Cole as a replacement for the Frenchman, now that he had at long last been removed from the mint. Whether or not Cole knew his approach was a long shot, its rejection appears to have been the signal for his withdrawl from the mint.

The mint was clearly of enormous importance in Humphrey Cole's career. Indeed for 15 years it was his main career, providing him with accommodation and a regular salary. He was trained by experienced mint personnel in the making of coining dies, and presumably also in the making of the tools used in this. His post involved intricate working in metal on the smallest scale, to produce tiny letter punches and design features, and placing these with accuracy and evenness. Above all, his post also allowed him the time to perfect his skills and employ them on the instruments which made his name.

Acknowledgements

This paper owes virtually everything to the research of a small number of historians and numismatists who have concentrated on the late-Tudor period. Chief among them is Christopher Challis, whose work in this area is all-pervading and inescapable.

Bibliography

Borden, D.G. and Brown, I.D., 'The Milled Coinage of Elizabeth I', *British Numismatic Journal* 53 (1983), pp. 108-32.

Brown, I.D., 'Some Notes on the Coinage of Elizabeth I with Special Reference to her Hammered Silver', *British Numismatic Journal* 28 (1958), pp. 568-603.

Brown, I.D. and Comber, C.H., 'Portrait Punches Used on the Hammered Coinage of Queen Elizabeth I', *British Numismatic Journal* 58 (1988), pp. 90-95.

Carlyon-Britton, R., 'An Early Example of 'Mass-Production' of Coin Dies', Seaby's *Coin and Medal Bulletin* (1953), p. 325.

Challis, C.E., 'Mint Officials and Moneyers of the Tudor Period', *British Numismatic Journal* 45 (1975), pp. 51-76.

Challis, C.E., *The Tudor Coinage* (Manchester 1978).

Challis, C.E., Presidential Address: 'The Introduction of Coinage Machinery into the Royal Mint by Eloy Mestrell', part 1, *British Numismatic Journal* 59 (1989), pp. 256-62.

Challis, C.E. (ed.), *A New History of the Royal Mint* (Cambridge 1992).

Cook, B.J., 'The Pinchbeck Treasure Trove', *Numismatic Chronicle* 151 (1991), pp. 183-98.

Craig, Sir John, *The Mint* (Cambridge 1953)

Goldman, P.H.J., 'Eloye Mestrelle and the Introduction of the Mill and Screw Press into English Coinage circa 1561-75', *Spink*'s *Numismatic Circular* 82 (1974), pp. 422-7.

Gunther, R.T., 'The Great Astrolabe and Other Scientific Instruments of Humphrey Cole', *Archaeologia* 26 (1927), pp. 273-317.

Hawkins, E. *Medallic Illustrations of the History of Great Britain and Ireland to the Death of George II*, vol. 1. London.

Stewart, B.H.I.H. 1964. 'Second Thoughts on Medieval Die-Output', *Numismatic Chronicle* 7th ser. 4 (1885), pp. 293-303.

Symonds, H., 'Engravers of the Tudor and Stuart Period', *Numismatic Chronicle* 4th ser. 13 (1913), pp. 349-77.

Symonds, H., 'The Mint of Queen Elizabeth and Those Who Worked There', *Numismatic Chronicle* 76 (1916), pp. 61-105.

CATALOGUES

The Scientific Instruments

Silke Ackermann

While nothing specifically identifiable survives from Humphrey Cole's tenure at the Mint, we are extremely fortunate in having 26 spectacular instruments signed by the most renowned maker of sixteenth-century England. Of these, 23 have been brought together for the exhibition - the first of its kind in the British Museum, and the three remaining pieces[1] are fully described in the catalogue. This represents a unique opportunity to study the work of this extraordinary maker and to appraise the surviving pieces for the first time as an oeuvre. Even at the time of their construction they were separated by years and it is very likely, therefore, that not even in Cole's workshop could they have been seen together as a group.

Although the majority of the instruments are dated 1574 and 1575, the total output spans a lifetime, the earliest instrument dating from 1568, the last from 1590.

It is perhaps significant that all the surviving instruments were made of metal - (gilt) brass or silver - and were therefore far from commonplace even when they were first made. While contemporary makers also supplied wooden instruments, it seems that the range offered by Humphrey Cole did not include this cheaper variety: Scales, compasses, and sundry sorts of Geometricall instruments in metall, are to be had in the house of Humfrey Cole, neere unto the North dore of Paules, and at the house of John Bull at the Exchange gate; in wood, at John Reades in Hosier Lane, at James Lockerfons dwelling neere the Conduite at Dowegate, and at John Reynolds at Tower Hill.[2]

The instruments by Humphrey Cole cover the whole range of 'mathematical instruments': sundials and nocturnals for telling the time at day and night, astrolabes and a 'universal instrument' for the same purpose and additionally for measuring the positions of heavenly bodies, and astronomical compendia which consist not only of sundials and nocturnals, but also provide a wide variety of tables with latitude lists, perpetual calendars, and information for astrological use. Besides these instruments mainly for astronomical and astrological purposes, there are those which are used for surveying and taking measurements such as the theodolites, the plane table alidade and the folding rules, the latter also providing tables for use in gunnery and trade.

As many abbreviations and symbols as possible have been transliterated to facilitate reading the catalogue. The following characters have been used to indicate what is written in the original:

[ ] a symbol for the zodiacal signs or planets has been transliterated into words.

< > an abbreviation given has been transliterated into letters

{ } no abbreviation sign is to be found on the instrument, but the word could nevertheless be extended fully by comparison with other inscriptions

( ) explanatory notes

Most special terms have been explained alongside the descriptions, and a glossary at the end of this section of the catalogue provides further information.

Acknowledgements

It would not have been possible to mount this exhibition and to write the accompanying catalogue without the help of the staff of all the lending institutions, and the most generous advice and support I have received from my colleagues: Peter Barber, Markus Barow, Paul Buck, Andrew Burnett, Ian Carradice, Gloria Clifton, Barrie Cook, Jeremy Evans, Rob van Gent, Hester Higton, Stephen Johnston, Nadine Maquet, Mara Miniati, Alison Morrison-Low, Allen Simpson, Peter Stringer, David Thompson, Pam Thompson, Kenneth Timbers, Josephine Turquet and all those whose names I may have omitted inadvertently.

Notes

[1] The instruments in Berlin, Florence and Liège (catalogue nos. 6, 15 and 20).

[2] E. Worsop, *A Discoverie of Sundrie Errours*, London 1582.

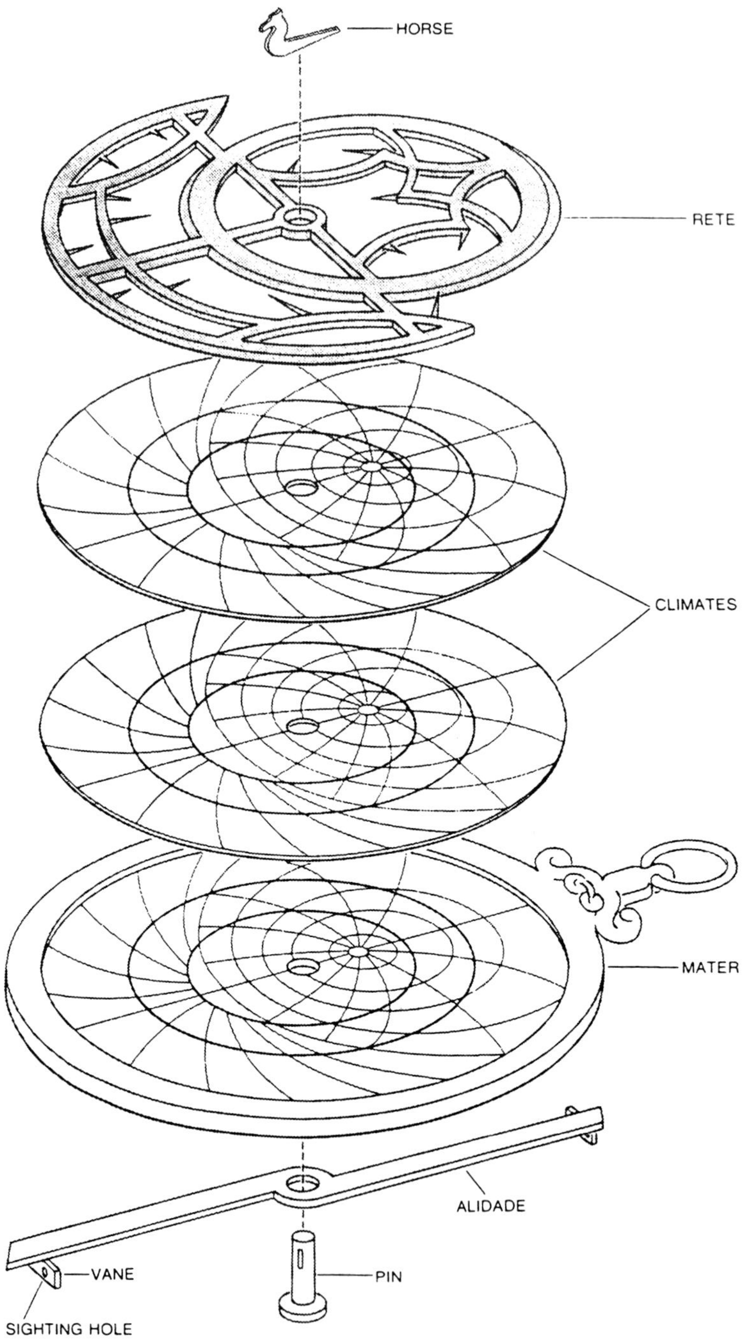

Figure 4 An exploded view of an astrolabe. Reproduced by kind permission of J.D. North from his article 'The Astrolabe', *Scientific American 230 (Jan. 1974), pp. 96-106.*

Astrolabes

The planispheric astrolabe is a two-dimensional model of the celestial sphere in relation to the earth, based on the assumption that the earth is in the centre of the universe. It is a multifunctional instrument which can be used to tell the time, to determine the length of day and night, to demonstrate the movements of the heavenly bodies, as well as for surveying and for astrological purposes (see Figure 4). Essentially the instrument consists of a celestial part (the 'rete'), a terrestrial part (the 'plates', also called 'climates'), and a thick brass plate with a rim (the 'mater'), an index on the front (the 'rule') and another on the back with additional sights (the 'alidade'). These parts are held together by a pin and a wedge called a 'horse'.

The rete is a skeletal brass disc representing the ecliptic and some prominent stars. The ecliptic is marked with the names of the zodiacal signs and a corresponding degree scale. The rete rotates over the plates.

The plates are brass discs with a little tongue at one side to prevent them from moving once in place. They are laid out for different latitudes normally indicated on the plates. This is due to the fact that the celestial movements we see depend on the latitude of the place of observation. Each plate has several engraved circles and lines which are normally the following:

- The circles for the tropics and the equator.
- The almucantars (circles of equal altitude parallel to the horizon) and the azimuths (lines of direction). The lowest of the almucantars represents the observer's horizon, on Flemish and Flemish-influenced instruments sometimes called the 'horizon obliquus'. The latitude for which these lines are constructed are marked on each plate, sometimes with the names of corresponding cities. The almucantars and azimuths are local co-ordinates defining the location of a heavenly body in relation to the observer's horizon. They can be compared to latitude and longitude on earth defining the location of a place in relation to the equator.
- The twilight curve: a line engraved on some plates 18° below the horizon, marking the beginning of the morning twilight and the end of evening twilight.
- Unequal hour lines: 12 lines normally drawn below the horizon representing hours in a system where the time between sunrise and sunset and the time between sunset and sunrise is divided into 12 'hours' each.
- Astrological Houses: on some plates a division of the sky into 12 parts for astrological purposes is marked. These lines overlap some of the hour lines and can easily be confused. There are different systems for the division, the most usual one being of Islamic origin, but commonly associated with the fifteenth-century astronomer Regiomontanus, where the boundary lines begin at the north point of the observer's horizon.

The plates and the rete are housed in a container of the same material, called the mater. The mater consists of a brass plate with a rather thick rim rivetted or soldered to it. To the mater a suspension apparatus is fixed to a protruding part called the throne. The throne can have different shapes which can be rather distinctive for particular makers.

The rim has usually both a 360-degree scale and a 24- hour scale. The inside edge of the rim has a small aperture to accommodate the tongues of the plates. The mater, i.e. the inside of the container, can be either left blank, be inscribed for another plate or be engraved with a 'quadratum nauticum'. The latter is a graduated square frequently found on Flemish and Flemish-influenced instruments which allows the sailor to find, without calculation, the course between two points of which the latitude and longitude are known. Some astrolabes have the names of the winds inscribed on the edge of the rim.

The back of the astrolabe contains several scales needed for the use of the instrument, but also serves as space for further information which could also be deduced from tables. The main features are:

- A 360-degree altitude scale.
- A calendrical scale (either for the Julian or the Gregorian calendar) with the names of the months and day divisions.
- A zodiacal scale with the names of the signs and sometimes their symbols with a degree scale.
- A shadow square which is normally to the base 12 and further divided. The horizontal scale is called 'Umbra versa' (for shadows cast by a horizontal gnomon), the vertical scale is called 'Umbra recta' (for shadows cast by a vertical gnomon).
- An horary quadrant for unequal hours.

The alidade is a brass bar usually the same length as the diameter of the instrument. It normally has sights for making observations.

The rule can have either the length of the radius or of the diameter of the astrolabe. It rotates over the front and acts as an index, sometimes with a declination scale.

The fixing normally consists of a pin which goes through the central holes in the mater, the plates and the rete. The pin is held in place by a small metal piece which often had the shape of a stylized horse's head and is therefore called the 'horse'.

1 Astrolabe Figure 5 on Plate I

British Museum, London

inv. no. MLA 1855,12-1.223

Signed and dated: Humfrey Cole 1574

Gilt brass; diameter 88 mm

This small astrolabe is an excellent example of Humphrey Cole's fine craftsmanship and shows clearly the Flemish influence on early English makers: star names are given with their magnitudes and their corresponding planetary temperaments and the plates have both the 'Horizon rectus' and the 'Horizon obliquus'. The mater has markings for a Quadratum Nauticum and the back shows the universal projection as described by Gemma Frisius in his treatise on the '*Catholic Astrolabe*'.

It is possible that the instrument once belonged to Henry, Prince of Wales (1594-1612) as an inscription in a later hand on the mater suggests, but the case bearing the monogram and the coat of arms of Henry is very likely to be a nineteenth-century addition.

The rim of the mater is marked with an equal 24-hour scale and a 360-degree scale. The hour scale is numbered twice I - XII starting at the throne. The degree scale is graduated anticlockwise starting at 6 o'clock on the right-hand side, numbered by 10, divided to 2 by alternate shading and subdivided to 1. The limb is rivetted to the back plate. The inside of the limb has a recess slightly to the left of 12 o'clock to accommodate the tongues of the plates.

The mater is engraved with, and marked as, a 'Quadratum Nauticum', the compass with 32 points filling the centre of the square. The edges of the square are each divided into scales of 90°, numbered by 10° and subdivided to 5°. On top of the squares are the inscriptions 'Longi{tudo} mi{nor} sive Occi{dentalior}' on the left and 'Longi{tudo} ma{ior} seu Orie{ntalior}' on the right; on the left-hand side are the inscriptions 'Lati{tudo} mi{nor} vel austr{alior}' on the left and 'Lati{tudo} ma{ior} aut Bore{alior}' on the right, each separated by entwined lines.

The instrument is signed 'Made by Humfrey Cole' and dated '1574' on the right- hand side of the square. The base is inscribed 'AD Henr{ici} Princ{ipis} Magni Brittan{iae}' in a different hand.

The outside edge of the limb is inscribed clockwise with the names of 13 stars and the corresponding planetary temperaments according to Ptolemy. Some star names are abbreviated so that instead of the names of the zodiacal signs the symbols are given (the modern identifications are given in brackets):

A Aquila [Mars Jupiter]	(α Aquilae)
B Lanceat<or> [Jupiter Mars]	(α Boötes)
C Cor Leonis [Mars Jupiter]	(α Leonis)
D Oculus [Tauri] [Mars]	(α Tauri)
E Can<is> ma<ior> [Jupiter Mars]	(α Canis Maioris)
F Spica Virginis [Venus Mars]	(α Virginis)
G Cor Scorpionis [Jupiter Mars]	(α Scorpii)
H Lucida hyd{rae} [Saturn Venus]	(α Hydrae)
I Arcturus [Jupiter Mars]	(α Boötes)
K Umbilic<us> Andr{omedae} [Venus]	(β Andromedae)
L Orion [Mars Mercury]	(α Orionis)
M Crus Aquarii [Mercury Saturn]	(α Aquarii)

Cole obviously mentions Arcturus twice: with this name and with the alternative form 'Lanceator'.

The throne consists of two foliate scrolls and an inset compass under a movable lid. Both the lid and the reverse of the compass are engraved with an armillary sphere.

The rete has flame-shaped star pointers. The circle for the tropic of Capricorn ends with the head and tail of a dragon. The names of 13 stars are given, mostly with their magnitude indicated by arabic numerals, as follows:

UMBILICUS ANDROMEDAE 3	β ANDROMEDAE
OCULUS [TAURI] 1	α TAURI
SINISTER PES ORIONIS 1	β ORIONIS
CANIS MAIOR 1	α CANIS MAIOR
LUCIDA HIDRAE 2	α HYDRAE
COR LEONIS 1	α LEONIS
SPICA VIRGINIS 1	α VIRGINIS
ARCTURU<S>	α BOÖTES
COR [SCORPIONIS]	α SCORPII
AQUILA 2	α AQUILAE
HUMER<US> EQUI MA{IORIS} 2	β PEGASI
CRUS [AQUARII]	α AQUARII

The ecliptic is marked with the usual Latin names of the zodiacal signs, some of which are abbreviated. Each sign has a 30 degree scale, numbered by 10 and divided to 2 on the outside edge of the ecliptic.

There are four plates, one of which is completely devoid of markings. Two plates are marked on both sides with the circles for the equator (marked 'AEQUATOR') and the tropics (marked 'Tro{picus} Can{cri}' and 'Tropicus Capricorni'), azimuths for every 10° (numbered by 10°), the almucantars for every 10° (numbered by 10°), the lines for the unequal hours (numbered 1 - 12), and the markings for the astrological houses in the manner of Regiomontanus, numbered I - XII. The 'Horizon obliquus' and the 'HORIZON RECTUS' are indicated and marked. An engraved twilight curve is marked 'Linea Crepusculi'. These two plates are laid out and marked for the following latitudes:

1a) 51;30°
1b) 52;30°
2a) 53;40°
2b) 55°.

The third plate has markings for the 'Horizontale Catholicum' and is named as such. The horizons are numbered by 10°. The 'Linea meridi{onalis}', the 'Equinoctialis' and the 'HORIZON RECTUS' are indicated. On the back of this plate are markings which are usually found on the back of an astrolabe which here takes the form of a universal projection (see below). On the outside are the following circular calendrical scales (from the outside):

1) The signs of the zodiac marked with the usual Latin names (some abbreviated) and the symbols anticlockwise

starting at the east-west line, each sign with a 30° scale, numbered by 10 and divided to 2 by alternate shading.
2) The months of the year with the usual Latin names (some abbreviated), numbered 1 - 12. The equinoxes correspond to March 11 and September 14, the solstices with June 12 and December 12.
The bottom half of the vacant space inside these circles is taken up by a double shadow scale marked 'Umbra Versa' and 'Umbra Recta' to the base of 12 with division into 2 digits and subdivision into single digits. The top half contains an hour diagram for converting equal hours into unequal hours or vice versa; the unequal hours are marked I - XII, the equal hours 1 - 12 - 1 'HORAE ANTE ME{RIDIEI}' and 'HORAE POST MERI{DIEI}'. The equal hours are laid out in the form of segments of vertical hyperbolic spirals.
The back of the instrument is engraved with Gemma Frisius' universal projection with the positions of 6 stars marked. These stars are only referred to by the letters A to G which correspond with the stars shown on the outside of the limb (see above). The right ascension (α) and declination (δ) of six stars can be read off:

	α	δ
A Aquila	291	+7
B Lanceator	209	+21
C Cor Leonis	145	+13
D Oculus Tauri	62	+19
E Canis Maior	97	- 16
F Spica Virginis	196	- 9
G Cor Scorpionis	240	- 24

The ecliptic is marked with the symbols of the zodiacal signs. The outside is graduated four times 90° - 0° numbered by 10° and divided to 2° by alternate shading. The tropics are graduated 1 - 12.
Over the back moves a triple-jointed brachiolus mounted on a cursor (marked 'Cursor Brachiolum') which can be slid along a horizontal rule fixed to the pin (the fixing screw being a replacement). The cursor is irregularly graduated from the centre 0° - 90° on one edge and regularly graduated from the centre 0° - 100° on the other edge. The scales are numbered by 10° divided to 2° by alternate shading. The rule is graduated along both margins, starting at the top in the centre 0° - 90°, continuing 90° - 270° along the whole length of the bottom and 270° - 360° back on the top, numbered by 10° and divided to 2° by alternate shading. The alidade mounted on the front is pivoted on the central pin with what appears to be a unique fixing mechanism: the pin has a circular incision into which the alidade slides. The alidade itself consists of two layers: a solid bar to which the sighting vanes are fixed and two pincer-like arms which are pivoted to the solid bar in the centre. These arms are held in position when closed by two small studs. If the arms are slightly raised and turned the alidade can be lifted off. The engravings on the alidade are on the movable parts and give the 'HORAE OCCA{SUS} [SOLIS]' and 'HO{RAE} ORTUS [SOLIS]' one arm with the hours numbered 1 - 12. On the other arm are markings for the azimuths 0° - 30° for the 'LATI{TUDO} MERI{DIONALIS}' and 0° - 90° for the 'LATITUDO SEPTEN{TRIONALIS}', numbered by 10°.
The fitted case - probably a nineteenth-century addition - is covered with green velvet (now partially rubbed down to the black underlay) and lined on the inside with red velvet. All the hinges and fastenings are of silver. On the side hinge-plate, decorated with stars is written 'Inter omnes'; on the top hinge-plate is a five-pointed star overlaid with the letter M. Three silver mounts on the lid are crudely engraved as follows: 1. 'faelicitas Illius cresca<n>t in eternum'; 2. The initials 'HP', 'ICH DIEN' with three feathers; 3. 'Scientia virtusque Autoritas et' and 'virtus' and another illegible word on the edges.

Bibliography

Gunther, R.T., 'The Great Astrolabe and other Scientific Instruments of Humphrey Cole', *Archaeologia* 76, 1927, pp. 278-280.

Gunther, R.T., *The Astrolabes of the World II: The Western Astrolabes* (Oxford 1932), pp. 484-487, no. 306

Ward, F.A.B., *A Catalogue of European Scientific Instruments in the Department of Medieval and Later Antiquities of the British Museum* (London 1981), pp. 116-117, no. 336.

2 Astrolabe Figure 6
University of St. Andrews
Signed and dated: Humfridus Côle Londiniensis hoc instrumentum fabricavit 21 die Maij A<nn>o D<omi>ni 1575.
Brass; diameter 610 mm

The size of this very accurately inscribed instrument is rather unusual: it measures more than half a metre in diameter.
Only one original plate has survived, but a replacement plate is inscribed in a remarkably similar fashion to the original. This plate was executed by John Marke in the 1680s for the latitude 56° 25', i.e. St. Andrews. This is a rare occurrence of an astrolabe being used and adjusted to the owner's needs.
The rim of the astrolabe consists of several layers of brass rivetted to the backplate. It is marked with a 360-degree scale and a 24-hour scale. The degree scale is numbered anticlockwise from the west (90 degrees from the throne) by 5 and divided to 1 and ½. The hour scale is numbered twice anticlockwise I-IX with divisions to 10 and 1 minutes.
The inside of the rim has a recess at 12 o'clock to accommodate the tongues of the plates.
The mater is engraved with, and marked as, a 'Quadratum Nauticum' the compass with 32 points filling the centre of the square. The points are marked with the first letters e.g. 'N, NBE, NNE, NEBN, NE, NEBE, ENE, EBN, E'. north is additionally marked with a fleur-de-lis.

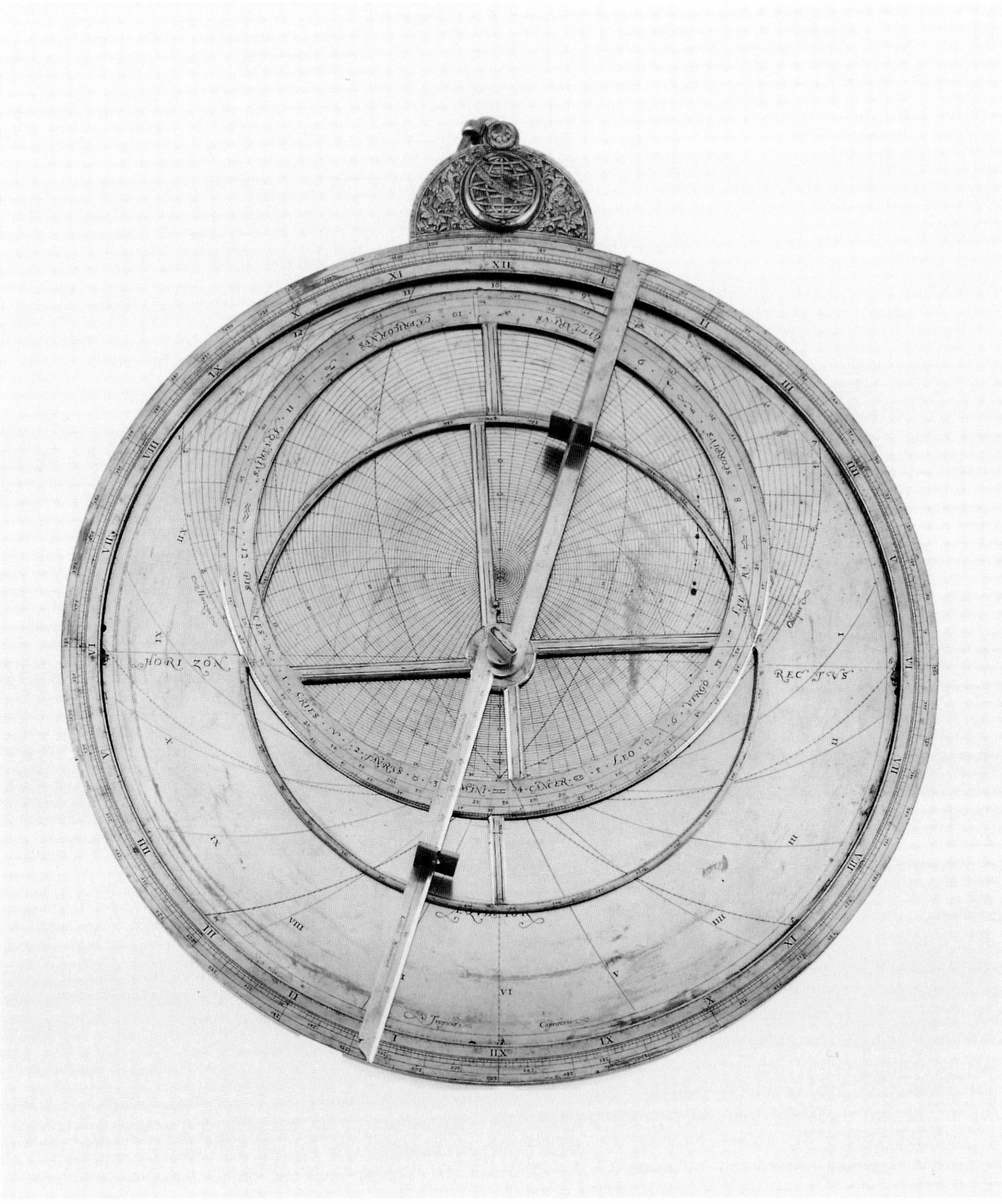

Figure 6 Astrolabe 1575 (catalogue no. 2). Reproduced by kind permission of the University of St. Andrews.

The four quarters are marked 'Latitudo minor uel Australior', 'Latitudo maior aut Borealior', 'Longitudo minor siue Occidentalior' and 'Longitudo maior seu Orientalior'. Each quarter has a degree scale 0 - 90, numbered by 5 and divided to 1.

On the right-hand side of the quadratum are the signature and the date 'Humfridus Côle Londiniensis hoc instrumentum fabricavit 21 die Maij A<nn>o D<omi>ni 1575'.

Between the scales and the compass in the centre the names of 16 winds are marked in Latin, Greek and Italian as follows (starting from the north clockwise):

Aparcticas	Bόρεas	Tramo<n>tana
Aquilo	Μέσησ	Griego tramo<n>tana
Griego		GRECO
Cacias	Καικίας	Griego levante
Subsolanus	Απηλιώτυς	Xaloq<ue> Levante
Vulturnus	Ευρα	Xaloq<ue> Levante
Xaloque		SYROCHO
Euroauster	Φοικικίας	Xaloque medio iorno
Auster	Vόπα	Medio iorno
Libonothus	Λιβονοθα	Medio iorno lebeche
Lebeche		LEBECCIO
Africus	Λίψ	Pomente Lebeche
Zephyrus	Ζέφοα	Pomente
Corus	Αργέςης	Pomente maestre
Maestrael		MAGISTRALIS
Circius	Ιάτυξ	Maestre tramo<n>{tana}

The semicircular throne is decorated with foliage and grapes issuing from a cornucopia. Inset in the centre of the front is a compass box (now empty), the lid of which is decorated with an armillary sphere with the symbols of the zodiac engraved.

The rete has no star pointers, but consists only of a frame for the ecliptic and the equator. The equator has a 360-degree scale, numbered anticlockwise by 10 (starting at 0° Aries), divided to 5, 1 and ½. It is marked with the usual Latin names of the zodiac and their symbols. The signs are numbered, starting with 1 for Aries. Each sign has a 30° scale, numbered by 5 and divided to 1 and ½.

The reverse of the rete is devoid of markings.

There are two plates, one of which has been engraved, on one side only, at a later date.

1a) 'Latitudo 52 0', marked with the hour lines (numbered I - XII), the astrological houses (numbered 1 - 12), the circles for the tropics and the equator (marked 'Tropicus Cancri', Tropicus Capricorni' and 'AEQUATOR'), the 'HORIZON RECTVS' and the 'Horizon Obliquus', azimuths for every 5°, numbered by 10° and almucantars for every single degree, numbered by 10°.

1b) marked with horizons between 0° and 90° in single degrees, numbered by 5°. The 'Equinoctialis', the 'Tropicus Capricorni', the 'HORIZON RECTVS' and the 'Linea Meridiana' are marked.

2a) this plate for 'Latitudo 56 25', which 'John Marke fecit', is inscribed with the astrological houses (numbered 1 - 12), the circles for the tropics and the equator (marked 'Tropicus Cancri', Tropicus Capricorni' and 'AEQUATOR'), the 'HORIZON RECTVS' and the 'Horizon Obliquus', azimuths for every 5°, numbered by 10° and almucantars for every single degree, numbered by 10°.

2b) blank.

The back is engraved with the universal stereographic projection of Gemma Frisius. The right ascension (α) and declination (δ) of 20 stars can be read off (here given in decimal notation). The modern identification is given in brackets.

	α	δ	
Cap. Medusae	40.4	+39.8	(β Persei)
Extre. Eridan.	43.1	-40.8	(θ Eridani)
Hircus	71.7	+45.2	(αAurigae)
Sinis. pes Orio.	73.0	-9.2	(β Orionis)
Dex. hu. Ori.	83.2	+6.2	(α Orionis)
Canopus	93.5	-51.7	(α Carinae)
Canis Ma.	97.0	-15.9	(α Canis Maioris)
Apollo	106.8	+32.2	(α Geminorum)
Canis mi.	109.5	+6.1	(α Canis Minoris)
Hercules	110.2	+28.5	(β Geminorum)
Cor [Leo]	145.8	+13.7	(α Leonis)
Benan.	170.7	+51.2	(η Ursae Maioris)
Cauda [Leo]	171.5	+16.5	(β Leonis)
Spica	196.0	-8.9	(α Virginis)
Arcturus	209.1	+22.0	(α Boötes)
Luci. Coronae	228.8	+28.5	(α Coronae Borealis)
Cor [Sco]	240.8	-24.9	(α Scorpii)
Lu. Lyrae	275.1	+38.7	(α Lyra)
Vult. Volans	291.8	+7.6	(α Aquilae)
Fomalhaut	338.5	-33.5	(α Piscis Austrini)

On the outside is a degree scale, marked anticlockwise (starting at the throne) 0 - 90, 0 - 90, 0 - 90, 0 - 90, numbered by 5 and divided to 1 and ½.

The brachiolus, cursor and rule needed to use this projection are missing.

The alidade is counterchanged with two sights and has bevelled tips. One arm is marked with a declination scale: 'Latitudo Meridionalis' from 0 - 80, numbered by 10 and divided to 5 and 1, and 'Latitudo Septentrionalis', numbered by 10 and divided to 5 and 1.

Bibliography

Gunther, R.T., 'The Great Astrolabe and Other Scientific Instruments of Humphrey Cole', *Archaeologia* 76 (1927), pp. 274-278.

Gunther, R.T., *The Astrolabes of the World, vol. II: The Western Astrolabes* (Oxford 1932), pp. 488-492.

Macdonald, Angus and A.D. Morrison-Low (eds), *A Heavenly Library: Treasures from the Royal Observatory's Crawford Collection* (Edinburgh 1994), p. 33.

The St. Andrew's Astrolabes. The Royal Scottish Museum. Special Exhibition Summer 1959.

Wray, E.M., Historical Scientific Instruments from the Collection of the Department of Physics, University of St. Andrews (St. Andrews 1984).

Universal Instrument

With this unusual instrument, of which no other example has come to light, the celestial co-ordinates of a heavenly body can be determined both in horizontal and equatorial co-ordinate systems. It can further be used to tell the time in equal hours.

A similar instrument was described by Martin Cortes in his *Breve Compendio de la Sphera y la Arte de Navegar* in 1551. This text was translated into English by Richard Eden as *The Arte of Navigation* and printed by Richard Jugge in 1572. Cole knew Jugge very well, as is demonstrated by the fact that he engraved a map for Jugge's *Bishop's Bible* of 1572 (catalogue no. 27) and made a very elaborate astronomical compendium for him (catalogue no. 10). It is thus very likely that Cortes' text was known to Cole when he constucted this instrument.

Figure 7 Martin Cortes' 'Instrument by the whiche ... is knowen the altitude of the Pole and the houre it is', English translation printed by Richard Jugge 1572 (British Library c.31.c.13). Reproduced by kind permission of the British Library.

3 Universal Instrument — Figure 8

St. Andrews University

Signed and dated: Humfrey Côle 1582

Brass; overall height 445 mm, overall width 360 mm

The instrument has a stand, similar to those found on globes, with an inset compass and a horizon ring. The stand supports an hour ring and a meridian ring attached to each other and to the four cardinal points of the horizon ring. Within the rings is a circular plate engraved in a similar way, but not identical, to the markings to be found on an 'Organum Ptolemai' with a movable alidade. The upper part of the instrument can be removed. The stand consists of a central base plate with four holes which may have been used to fix the instrument to a sturdy base.

The horizon ring is supported by a semicircle which itself has two continuous curved supports with a foot at each end, set at right-angles to each other and screwed to the base. Each foot is marked with cuts (I to IIII) which may have been used to identify their correct position on the base plate. The base is executed in a somewhat crude manner.

A compass bowl is fixed to the base plate, the compass card being marked with the four cardinal points with fleur-de-lis for north. The inside edge of the compass bowl has a degree scale 90 - 0 - 90 - 0 - 90, numbered by 2.

Descending from the central point of the stand is an open quatrefoil bracket with an up-standing point at the centre which registers with a plumb, the latter most likely a replacement.

The horizon ring has a semicircular protrusion on the outside at each of the four cardinal points; the ring itself has a rectangular slot at the same points. The slots at north and south are open. The ring is graduated 0° - 360° starting at north, numbered by 10 and divided to 1. Thirty-two directions are indicated with their first letters such as 'N, NBE, NEBN, NE, NEBE, ENE, EBN' etc. The markings for west (W) and east (+) have been partially destroyed by the above mentioned slots.

Attached to the horizon ring at east and west is an hour ring which is also fixed to the meridian ring at the east and west points. One side of the hour ring is marked with a 24-hour scale and a 360-degree scale. The hour scale is numbered clockwise twice I - XII, the degree scale is numbered by 10 and divided to 1.

The reverse is marked with a 12-hour scale, numbered VI - XII - VI, and a degree scale 0 - 90 - 0 - 90 - 0, numbered by 10 and divided to 1.

The meridian ring has a degree scale starting at the North Pole (marked 'polus' with a brass pointer) 90 - 0 - 90 - 0 - 90, numbered by 10 and divided to 1.

Where the hour ring and the meridian ring are fixed to each other there are spikes which slide through a cut-out in the horizon ring when the meridian ring is moved to set it to the appropriate latitude.

Fixed to the poles of the meridian ring is a circular disc with markings on the upper side. These look very similar to the face of an 'Organum Ptolemai': the edge is marked with a degree scale 90 - 0 - 90 - 0 - 90, numbered by 10 and divided to 5 and 1. Between 23 ½ degrees north and south of the equator is a declination scale for the zodiacal signs, each with a 30° scale and divided to 10°. The signs are indicated with their usual Latin names on one side and with their symbols on the other. Curved lines which in one application would serve as Meridian lines are drawn, but not labelled as hour lines as they would be on the 'Organum'.

Additionally the 'Polus Zodiaci', the 'Polus Arcticus' and 'Polus Antarcticus' with the 'Axis', the 'Stella Polaris', the 'Tropicus Cancri' and 'Tropicus Capricorni', and the 'Aecliptica' and the 'Aequinoctialis' are marked. On the top right-hand side next to the polar star is the signature and the date 'Humfrey Côle fecit 1582'.

The reverse of the plate is devoid of markings; a brass ring supports the disc.

A counterchanged alidade with two sighting vanes, fixed with a pin and a pierced plate, rotates over the plate.

In any application the instrument has to be aligned in an exact north - south direction using the compass in the base.

To determine horizontal co-ordinates, the meridian ring has to be set to latitude 90°, so that the axis on which the plate rotates is perpendicular to the horizon ring and directed to the zenith.

Using the alidade to observe a particular heavenly body the altitude can be read off the degree scale on the rim of the disc, and the azimuth can be read off the degree scale on the horizon ring.

To determine equatorial co-ordinates the meridian ring has to be set to the appropriate latitude. Using the alidade to observe a particular heavenly body, the declination can be read off the degree scale on the disc, while the hour angle (measured in hours either from the north or south meridian, is read off the equatorial ring (i.e. the hour ring). The right ascension, measured in hours from the first point of Aries, can be obtained from the hour angle if the solar position and the hour of the day are known.

The solar position can only be obtained from published tables, while the hour can be determined with the instrument itself.

To tell the time in equal hours from the sun's altitude, the meridian ring is set to the appropriate latitude and the disc is aligned with the sun. The position of the plate along the hour ring then indicates the time in equal hours.

Additionally the solar declination can be obtained by sighting the sun through the alidade and using the declination scale on the rim of the disc.

The use of the 'Organum Ptolemai' inscribed on the disc remains obscure.

Bibliography

Gunther, R.T., 'The Great Astrolabe and Other Scientific Instruments of Humphrey Cole', *Archaeologia* 76 (1927), pp. 274-278.

Macdonald, Angus and A.D. Morrison-Low (eds), *A Heavenly Library: Treasures from the Royal Observatory's Crawford Collection* (Edinburgh 1994), p. 29.

Reflections: From Alchemy to Astrophysics. An Exhibition of Historic Scientific Instruments from the School of Physics and Astronomy at the University of St. Andrews (St. Andrews 1996).

Wray, E.M., *Historical Scientific Instruments from the Collection of the Department of Physics, University of St. Andrews* (St. Andrews 1984).

Figure 8 Universal instrument 1582 (catalogue no. 3). Reproduced by kind permission of the University of St. Andrews.

Horizontal Sundials

Horizontal sundials are the most common type of sundial and as such can still be found in gardens and public parks. A horizontal dial is restricted to a particular latitude, i.e. it only tells the time correctly at a particular location. The simplest form consists of a horizontal plate inscribed with markings for the common hours onto which a shadow is cast by a triangular gnomon whose straight edge has to be parallel with the axis of the earth when the dial is properly aligned in a north-south direction. If the latitude for which the dial was designed is not marked on the plate, it can be determined by measuring the angle which the gnomon forms with the plate.
Both surviving horizontal dials by Cole are simple garden sundials and - judging from their patinated surfaces - were obviously used as such.

4 Horizontal Sundial Figure 9
Museum of the History of Science, Oxford
inv. no. 51,646 (previously Lewis Evans collection 232)
Signed and dated: H Côle 1579
Brass; dial plate 180 x 180 mm

A horizontal dial intended for use in the garden. Four holes suggest that it was fixed to a stand or pedestal.
The dial is marked for common hours, numbered VIII - XII - IV and divided to half-hours. The gnomon is set for *c.* 52°, a value close to the latitude of London.
A decorated compass rose in the centre of the hour scale is marked with the eight principal directions as 'N, NE, E, SE, S, SW, W, NW'.
The name of the owner, 'Sur Henry darcy', is engraved beside the south point in the hour circle. Darcy was knighted by the Earl of Leicester on 21 August 1565 in Kenilworth Castle.
The surface of the dial has been scratched with initials and names.

Bibliography

Gunther, R.T., 'The Great Astrolabe and other Scientific Instruments of Humphrey Cole', *Archaeologia* 76 (1927), pp.273-317, esp. p. 300.

5 Horizontal Sundial Figure 10 on Plate II
National Maritime Museum, Greenwich
inv. no. AST0390 (previously D.249)
Signed and dated: Humfrae Colle 1582
Brass; dial plate 127 x 130 mm

A horizontal dial intended for use in the garden. Four holes suggest that it was fixed to a stand or pedestal.
The dial is marked for common hours, numbered VIII - XII -IV and divided to half- and quarter-hours. The gnomon is set for *c.* 54°.
The instrument is signed and dated 'Humfrae Colle 1582' inside the hour circle.

Figure 9 Horizontal sundial 1579 (catalogue no. 4). Reproduced by kind permission of the Museum of the History of Science Oxford (photo Giles Hudson).

Quadrant Dials

These altitude dials by Humphrey Cole are very unusual examples of a sundial.

Each dial consists of a square horizontal plate, engraved with horary quadrants for equal and unequal hours for different latitudes, and a 45° triangular gnomon. Both sides of the dial contain tables and scales for astronomical and astrological purposes (see Figure 11).

In use, the dial is orientated so that the vertical edge of the right-angled gnomon casts a shadow parallel to one side of the dial plate. In this way the shadow of the inclined edge of the gnomon will indicate the altitude of the sun on the altitude scale of the quadrant. The time can be read off directly from the point where the shadow intersects the hour line for the appropriate date indicated by the position of the sun in the zodiac.

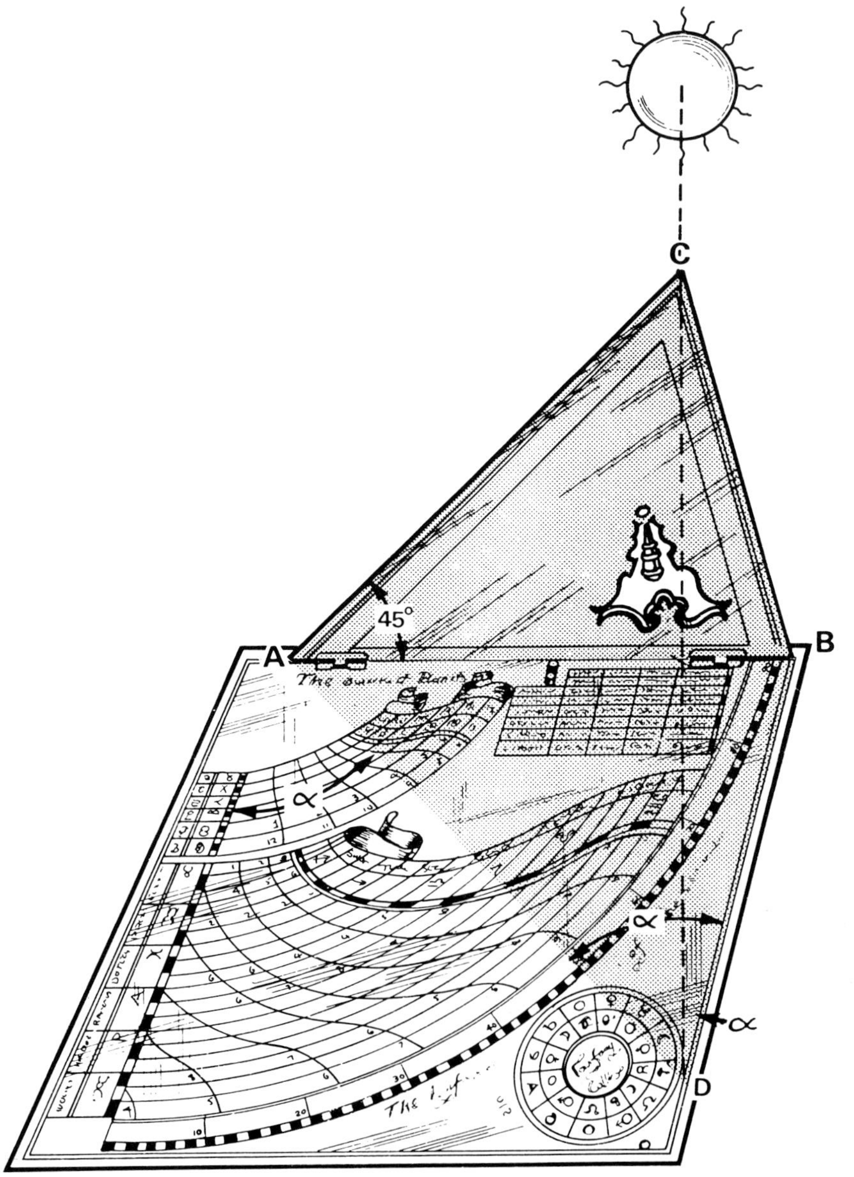

α = height of sun $\triangle ABD = \triangle CBD$

Figure 11 The use of the quadrant dial. Drawing reproduced by kind permission of Denys Vaughan from his article 'A Very Artificial Workman: The Altitude Sundials of Humphrey Cole', *Making Instruments Count. Essays on Historical Scientific Instruments presented to Gerard L'Estrange Turner, eds R.G.W. Anderson, J.A. Bennett, W.F. Ryan, (Aldershot, Variorum, 1993), pp. 191-200.*

6 Quadrant Dial — Figure 12

Kunstgewerbemuseum, Berlin

inv. no. K 4670
Signed and dated: Humfridus Côle Anglus 1574
Silver; dial plate 75 x 75 mm

Each side of the instrument is engraved with a large quadrant with two different sets of hour lines: equal hours on the outer (numbered 4 - 12 - 8 and divided to half-hours by dots), labelled 'Horae Diei', and unequal hours on the inner (numbered 1 - 6 - 12), labelled 'Horae planetarum'. The curved edge of the quadrant has a degree scale 0 - 90, labelled 'Altitudo Solis', numbered by 10 and divided to 5 and 1 by alternate shading. Both sets have scales of the zodiacal signs on both sides, marked with the symbols and the abbreviated Latin names. Arcs indicate the position of the sun in the zodiac at intervals of 30°. A table on the reverse (see below) allows the corresponding calendrical dates to be determined. The quadrant on the upper side is laid out for latitude 55° (marked 'G 55' at the tip of the quadrant), the underside for latitude 52°0' (marked 'G 52 M 0').

Outside the quadrant on the upper side is a circular perpetual Julian calendar with Dominical Letters for common and leap years (marked 'LITERA DO<M>' and 'BIS SIX'), Golden Numbers (marked 'AV NV') and Epacts ('CI EP') consisting of four rings and an inscription in the centre which reads 'Incipe ab Anno 1574', i.e. the table starts with this year. The first Dominical Letter is C, the Golden Number 17 and the Epact 7.

On the outside of the quadrant on the underside is a circular table showing the ruling planet for each hour of the day, indicated by the seven planetary symbols in 24 boxes, labelled 'Dominia planetarum' in the centre. At the right-hand sight close to the gnomon on the underside is an additional table with the dates of the sun's entry into a particular zodiacal sign. The table is labelled 'Introitus in 12 Signa'. The months are indicated with their first letter (marked 'M'), the day with the date (marked 'D'), the sun with the sun's effigy (marked 'So') and the signs with their symbols (marked 'Si'). The following dates can be read off:

Aquarius	11 January
Pisces	10 February
Aries	11 March
Taurus	11 April
Gemini	12 May
Cancer	12 June
Leo	14 July
Virgo	14 August
Libra	14 September
Scorpio	14 October
Sagittarius	13 November
Capricornus	12 December

Hinged to each side of the plate is a 45° triangular gnomon, held upright by a catch, with a decorative cut-out for the now missing plumb bob.

Bibliography

Hausmann, Tjark, *Alte Uhren*, (Berlin 1979), p. 54, no. 5.
Vaughan, Denys, 'A Very Artificial Workman: The Altitude Sundials of Humphrey Cole', *Making Instruments Count. Essays on Historical Scientific Instruments presented to Gerard L'Estrange Turner*, eds R.G.W. Anderson, J.A. Bennett, W.F. Ryan, (Aldershot, Variorum, 1993), pp. 191-200.

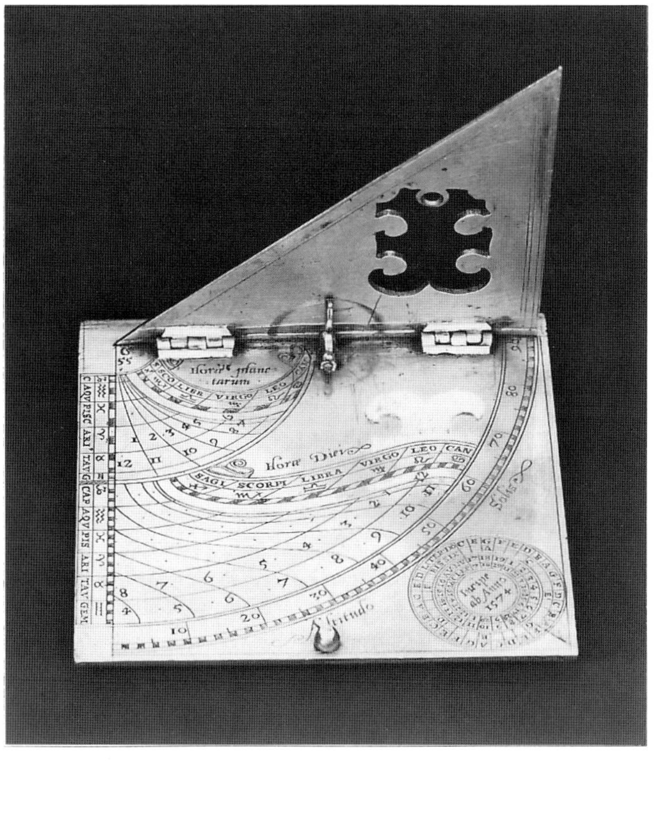

Figure 12 Upper side of the quadrant dial of 1574 (catalogue no. 6). Reproduced by kind permission of the Staatliche Museen zu Berlin - Preussischer Kulturbesitz Kunstgewerbemuseum (photo Arne Psille)

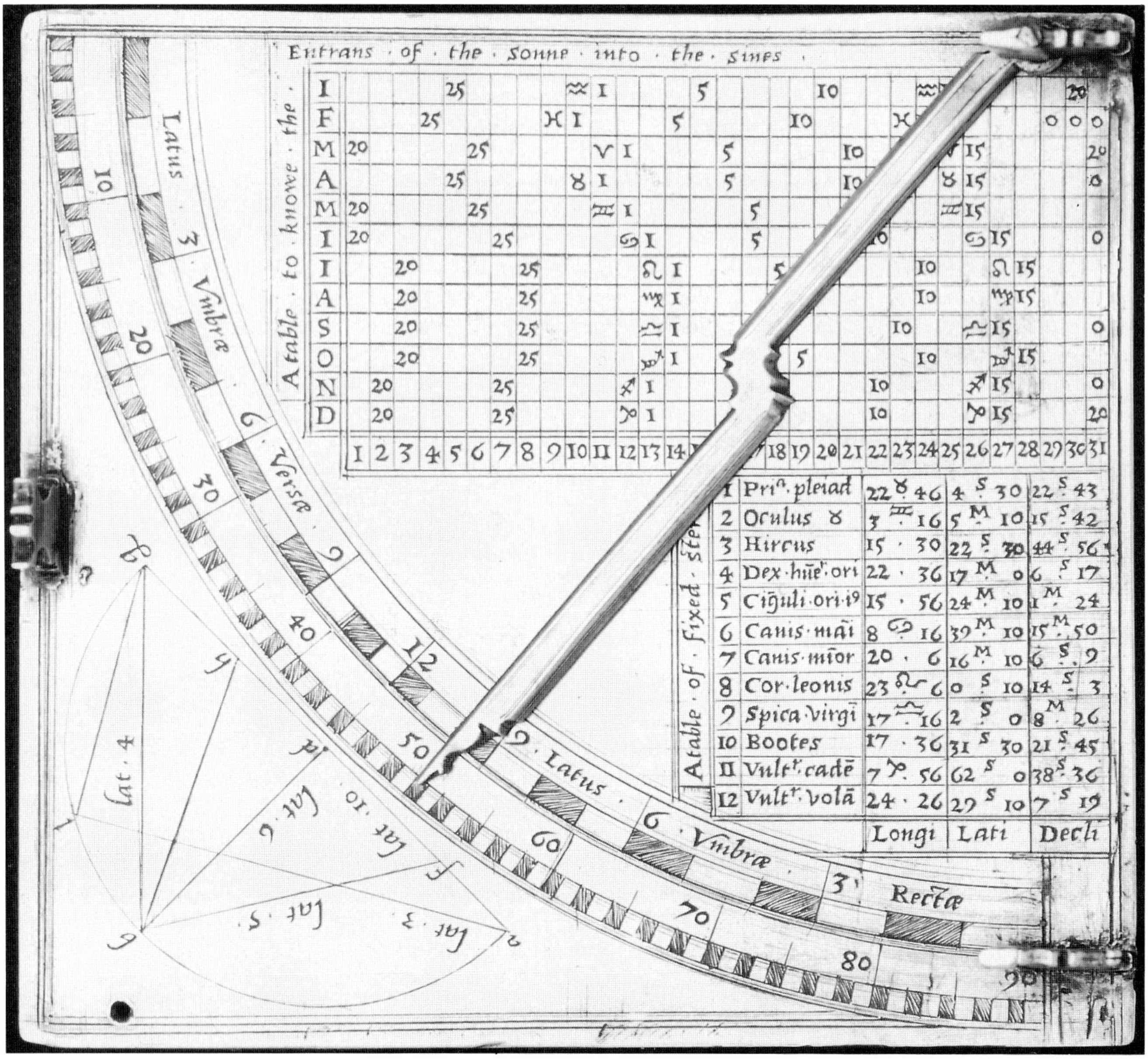

Figure 14 Underside of the undated quadrant dial (catalogue no. 7). Reproduced by kind permission of the Science & Society Picture Library.

7 Quadrant Dial Figure 13 on plate II, Figure 14
Science Museum, London
inv. no. 1985-100
Signed: humfray Colle
Undated
Silver; dial plate 73 x 78 mm

The upper side of the instrument is engraved with a large quadrant with two different sets of hour lines: equal hours on the outer (numbered at the largest arc 4 - 12 - 8, at the smallest arc 3 - 12 - 9), labelled 'The zodiac of oures', and unequal hours on the inner (numbered 1 - 6 - 12), labelled 'The oures of plenet<s>'. The curved edge of the quadrant has a degree scale 0 - 90, labelled 'The highte of the sonne', numbered by 10 and divided to 5 and 1 by alternate shading. Both sets have scales of the zodiacal signs on both sides, marked with the symbols and the abbreviated Latin names. Arcs indicate the position of the sun in the zodiac at intervals of 10°, the outermost representing the tropic of Cancer, the innermost representing the tropic of Capricorn and the one in the middle the equinoxes. A table on the reverse (see below) allows the corresponding calendrical dates to be determined.

The latitude for which the quadrant was constructed is marked as 'G/51 M/30' (i.e. 51°30', the latitude of London) on the left and right of a double circle opposite the tip of the quadrant. This circle shows the ruling planet for each hour of the day, indicated by the seven planetary symbols in 24 boxes, and is inscribed in the centre with the signature of the maker: 'humfray Colle'.

At the right-hand edge of the quadrant is a table with the Latin names of the cardinal points, the names of the four main winds, the four elements, the seasons, the humours and the ages of man, arranged under their common qualities as follows:

	Cali & Sicca	Cali & Hu<m>ida	Frig & Hu<m>ida	Frigid & Sicca
Mu<n>di reg	Orien	Meridi	Occide	Septent
Ve<n>ti Card	Eurus	Auster	Zephy	Boreas
Eleme<n>ta	Ignis	Aer	Aqua	Terra
Part An<n>i	Aestas	Ver	Hyems	Autum<n>us
4 Humor	Choler	Sa<n>gui	Phleg<m>a	Mela<n>chol
4 Aetate	Iuue<n>tu<s>	Adoles	Seniu<s>	Senectus

Cole follows here the well-known Galenic scheme, but deviates in the entries for the ages of man.
Hinged to one side of the plate is a 45° triangular gnomon held upright by a catch, with a decorative cut-out for the now missing plumb bob.
The underside of the instrument is engraved with a quadrant with two scales:
1) a degree scale 0 - 90, numbered by 10 and divided to 5 and 1 by alternate shading;
2) a shadow scale to the base 12, marked 'Latus Vmbrae Versae' and 'Latus Vmbrae Rectae', numbered by 3 and divided to 1 by alternate shading. This quadrant can be used together with a rigid silver plumb pivoted to one of the three feet, two of which act as sighting vanes when this side of the instrument is used. When not in use the plumb can be fixed to the other foot which acts as a sighting vane.
Within this quadrant are two tables: one to find the entry of the sun into a particular zodiacal sign, marked 'A table to knowe the Entrans of the Sonne into the sines', and one giving the longitude, latitude and declination of 12 named stars (with 's' for Septentrio, i.e. north, and 'M' for Meridies, i.e. south), marked 'A table of fixed sterres'.
Table 1 gives the names of the months by their first letters on the vertical scale, the days of the months on the horizontal scale, and the zodiacal signs indicated by their symbols. Each sign is divided to 5° numbered by 5. The following dates can be read off:

Aquarius	11 January
Pisces	10 February
Aries	12 March
Taurus	11 April
Gemini	12 May
Cancer	13 June
Leo	14 July
Virgo	14 August
Libra	14 September
Scorpio	14 October
Sagittarius	13 November
Capricornus	13 December

The dates for the sun's entry into Aries, Cancer and Capricorn deviate from the usual dates given by Cole, i.e. 11 March, 12 June and 12 December.

The second table gives the following information:

	Longi{tudo}	Lati{tudo}		Decli{natio}	
1 Pri^a pleiad	22.46 [Tauri]	4.30	S	22.43	S
2 Oculus [Tauri]	3.16 [Gemini]	5.10	M	15.42	S
3 Hircus	15.30	22.30	S	44.56	S
4 Dex hu<m>e^r ori{onis}	22.36	17.0	M	6.17	S
5 Ci<n>guli ori{on}i<s>	15.56	24.10	M	1.24	M
6 Canis mai{or}	8.16 [Cancer]	39.10	M	15.50	M
7 Canis mi<n>or	20.06	16.10	M	6.9	S
8 Cor leonis	23.06 [Leo]	0.10	S	14.03	S
9 Spica virgi<n>{is}	17.16 [Libra]	2.0	S	8.26	M
10 Bootes	17.36	31.30	S	21.45	S
11 Vult<ur> cade<n>{s}	7.56 [Capricornus]	62.0	S	38.36	S
12 Vult<ur> vola<n>{s}	24.26	29.10	S	7.19	S

The given stars can be identified as follows:

1	19 Tauri
2	α Tauri
3	α Aurigae
4	α Orionis
5	δ Orionis
6	α Canis Maioris
7	α Canis Minoris
8	α Leonis
9	α Virginis
10	α Boötes
11	α Lyrae
12	α Aquilae

Outside the arc of the quadrant is a semicircle inscribed with triangles marked 'lat.3, lat.4, lat.5, lat.6, lat.10' (where 'lat.' stands for 'latus', i.e. side) and the letters a, b, d, f, g, h and i. These represent the lengths of the sides of regular polygons drawn inside a circle of the same radius as the semi circle.
The instrument has a wooden case covered with tooled leather and lined with red baize. The underside is decorated with fleurs-de-lis in squares and a floral motif on the edges. On the top is a Tudor rose surrounded by floral motifs. The leather hinge is torn and one of the ring closures to fix the two hooks is missing.
As well as the use of the dial explained above, the altitude of the sun can also be measured using the quadrant on the underside of the instrument with the help of the sighting vanes and the plumb and the dial thus orientated.

Bibliography

Christie's South Kensington, London, Sale Catalogue, 13 December 1984, lot 219.
Higgins, Kathleen, 'An Elizabethan Quadrant-Dial in Silver by Humphrey Cole', *Connoisseur*, 125 (1950), pp. 118-119.
Vaughan, Denys , 'A Very Artificial Workman: The Altitude Sundials of Humphrey Cole', *Making Instruments Count. Essays on Historical Scientific Instruments presented to Gerard L'Estrange Turner*, eds R.G.W. Anderson, J.A. Bennett, W.F. Ryan, (Aldershot, Variorum, 1993), pp. 191-200.

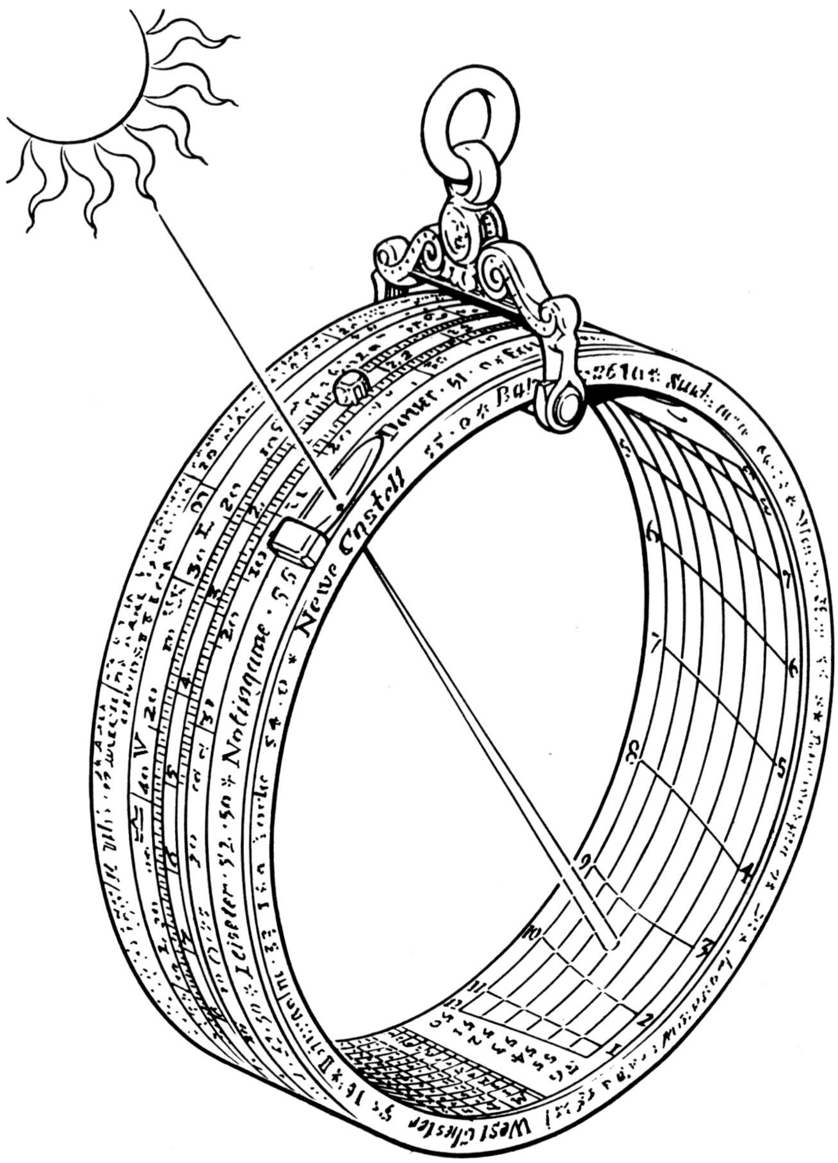

Figure 15 *Use of a ring dial (art work by Jim Farrant)*

Ring Dial

Ring dials are sundials in the form of a ring with a hole in a movable band to enable the sun's rays to indicate the time on a scale on the inside. They are fitted with a suspension apparatus with which they are held in a vertical position and then properly orientated (see Figure 15).

8 Ring Dial Figure 16 on Plate III
British Museum, London
inv. no. MLA 1905,6-8.1
Signed: H. Cole
c. 1575
Gilt brass; diameter 74 mm, width 22 mm

The only surviving ring dial made by Humphrey Cole is a particularly large and fine example. It has not only the essential hour markings and calendrical scales necessary to set it properly, but can be used at different latitudes and provides useful tables such as the dates of the sun's entry into the zodiacal signs, perpetual calendars, a list of latitudes of cities, a scale for the age of the moon and some astrological information.
This instrument consists of a ring with movable bands with pin holes and a movable suspension apparatus. It has on the inside markings for a ring dial for latitudes between 50° and 56°, tables for the entry of the sun into a particular zodiacal sign, and a perpetual calendar starting at 1575.
On the outside it is marked with a table with Saints' days and Christian feasts, planetary aspects, zodiacal and calendrical scales and a list of latitudes, which is continued on the outside edge.
In use the pin hole would be set to the appropriate time of the year and the right latitude on the scale on the inside.
The outside of the ring is marked anticlockwise with several scales as follows (starting at the top):
1) Table of Saints' days and Christian feasts (as well as the beginning and the end of the dog days) corresponding to the calendrical scale. The following dates are given:

for January
1 CIRCV 6 EPIPH 13 HILA 25 CŌ PĀ
for February
2 PVRIFI MARI 14 VALE 24 MAT
for March
12 GREGORI 25 ANVN MAR
for April
23 GEORGE 25 MARCVS
for May
1 PHILLI IACO 6 IOAN EVAN
for June
11 BARN 24 IO BAP 29 PETER PAVL
for July
6 DOGE BEGIN 22 MAG 25 IA APO
for August
1 PE VIN 17 DOG EN 24 BART 29 DEC IO
for September
8 NATI MARI 21 MAT 29 MICH
for October
13 EDWARD CON 18 LVC 28 SI IVD
for November
1 OMNI SAN 2 OM AN 30 ANDR
for December
6 NICO 8 CON MA 21 THO 25 NAT DO

2) A movable band is engraved with planetary aspects in words and symbols. A boss in the shape of a lunar crescent aids manual rotation.
CONIUNCTION
SEXTILE
QVADRINE
TRINALL
OPPOSITION
TRINALL
QVADRINE
SEXTILE

3) A fixed band is engraved with a zodiacal scale with the usual Latin names (indicated with the first letter) of the signs and their symbols. Each sign has a 30° scale, numbered by 10 and divided to 2 and 1.
4) Another movable band, with a boss to aid manual rotation, is inscribed with the age of the moon, numbered 1 - 29.
5) A fixed band is engraved with a Julian calendar scale with the usual Latin names of the months (indicated by their first letter). Each month has a corresponding date scale, numbered by 10 and divided to 2 and 1. December appears to have 31.25 days to indicate the leap year.
The equinoxes correspond to 11 March and 14 September, the solstices to 13 June and 12 December.
6) A third movable band, with a pin hole, has a list of cities with their latitudes (anticlockwise starting at the pinhole):

Notingame	53
Leiseter	52 50
Harford	52 50
Norwiche	52 30
Northampton	52 50
Bristo	51 20
Oxforde	51 50
London	51 34
Exiter	51 0
Dover	51 0

This list is continued on the outside edge:

Linckolne	53 15
West Chester	53 10
Louanium	50 58
Antwerpia	51 28
Winchester	51 0
Saulisburie	51 15
Barwick	56 0

Newe Castell	55 0
Yorke	54 0

On the inside of the ring are two circular perpetual calendars consisting of two circles each. Both are marked 'THIS TABLE BEGINETH AT A 1575 AND SO FOR EVER' in the centre. One calendar gives a list of Dominical Letters for common years and leap years, the other gives the Golden Numbers and Epacts as follows:

18	18	
19	29	(recte 11)
1	11	
2	22	
3	3	
4	14	
5	25	
6	6	
7	17	
8	28	
9	9	
10	20	
11	1	
12	12	
13	23	
14	4	
15	5	(recte 15)
16	26	
17	7	

Next to the latter is a scale with lines for the zodiacal signs (indicated by their symbols) for every 6° and latitude lines for latitudes between 50° to 56°.
The signature 'H Côle' appears at the bottom of this scale.

Next to this scale is a table for the entry of the sun into a particular zodiacal sign. The months are indicated by the first letter of their names, the sun by its effigy 12 times and the signs by their symbols. The columns are headed 'M' for the months, 'D' for the dates, 'SO' for the sun, and 'SI' for the signs. The following values can be read off:
The following dates can be read off:

11 January	Aquarius
10 February	Pisces
11 March	Aries
11 April	Taurus
12 May	Gemini
13 June	Cancer
14 July	Leo
14 August	Virgo
14 September	Libra
14 October	Scorpio
13 November	Sagittarius
12 December	Capricorn

The date given for the sun's entry into Cancer deviates from Cole's usual date 12 June.
Next to this table are oblique lines for the common hours numbered 4 - 12 - 9, and the lines for the latitudes between 50° and 56°.

Bibliography

Gunther, R.T., 'The Great Astrolabe and other Scientific Instruments of Humphrey Cole', *Archaeologia* 76 (1927), pp. 291-293.
Ward, F.A.B., *A Catalogue of European Scientific Instruments in the Department of Medieval and Later Antiquities of the British Museum* (London 1981), pp. 61 f., no. 161.

Nocturnal

Nocturnals are instruments used for telling the time at night from observations of fixed stars (see Figure 17).
The instrument consists of fixed calendrical and zodiacal scales against which the index of an hour scale on a volvelle has to be set for the appropriate date. The nocturnal is then held in an upright position and the Pole star is sighted through the hole in the centre. A second rotatable long index attached to the centre of the instrument is aligned with the pointer stars in the Great Bear and the time then read off from the point where the long index intersects with the hour scale. To facilitate reading at night the hours are further marked by small teeth.

9 Nocturnal Figure 18 on Plate III
British Museum, London
inv. no. MLA 1857,11-16.2
Signed: H Cole
Undated
Gilt brass; diameter 95 mm

This instrument consists of a circular disc with volvelles and indices on both sides. Attached to the disc is a small handle in the shape of a fleur-de-lis with a hole, on which are the initials 'W F'.
While one side works as a nocturnal, the other allows the prediction of high tide at a particular port.
The front of the disc is inscribed with a circular calendrical scale with the usual Latin names of the months, numbered 1 - 12 starting with January. Each month has the corresponding number of days (December has 31¼ to indicate the leap year), numbered by 10 and divided to 1. Within the centre of this scale is a volvelle with an hour scale, numbered twice anticlockwise 1 - 12. Teeth of alternating size indicate the full and half-hours. An index with a sun effigy at 12 o'clock allows this volvelle to be set to the correct date. The centre of the disc is engraved with scrollwork.
Over this volvelle rotates an index arm, labelled around the central hole 'STELLA POLARIS' and along the arm 'INDEX HORA NOCTIS'.
The signature of the maker 'H Cole' is inscribed on this arm.
The reverse has several circular scales as follows (from the outside):
1) a degree scale 0 to 360, numbered by 10 and divided to single degrees;
2) a 24-hour scale, numbered clockwise twice 1 - 12;
3) a compass rose of 32 points with the eight main directions indicated by their first letter(s), and north indicated by a fleur-de-lis. In the centre of this scale is a fixed disc with the age of the moon 1 - 30.
Over this disc rotates another volvelle with an index. A circular aperture shows the phases of the moon. The plate is marked with planetary aspects, but has not been completed.
The combination of scales 2 and 3 with the centre disc and volvelle allows the prediction of high tide at a particular port, provided the location of this place is known.

Bibliography

Gunther, R.T., 'The Great Astrolabe and other Scientific Instruments of Humphrey Cole', *Archaeologia* 76 (1927), pp. 293 f.
Ward, F.A.B., *A Catalogue of European Scientific Instruments in the Department of Medieval and Later Antiquities of the British Museum* (London 1981), pp. 74 f., no. 208.

Figure 17 The use of a nocturnal. Petrus Apian, Cosmographia, *edited by Gemma Frisius, Antwerp 1545. (British Library c.112.d.10). Reproduced by kind permission of the British Library.*

Plate I

Figure 5 Astrolabe 1574 (catalogue no. 1). Reproduced by kind permission of the Trustees of the British Museum.

Figure 24 Astronomical compendium 1579 (catalogue no. 14). Reproduced by kind permission of Christie's, London.

Figure 10 Horizontal sundial 1582 (catalogue no. 5). Reproduced by kind permission of the National Maritime Museum, London.

Figure 13 Upper side and case of the undated quadrant dial (catalogue no. 7). Reproduced by kind permission of the Science & Society Picture Library.

Plate III

Figure 16 Ring dial (catalogue no. 8). Reproduced by kind permission of the Trustees of the British Museum

Figure 18 Nocturnal (catalogue no. 9). Reproduced by kind permission of the Trustees of the British Museum

Plate IV

Figure 19   Astronomical compendium 1568 (catalogue no. 10). Reproduced by kind permission of the Museum of the History of Science, Oxford (photo Giles Hudson).

Figure 21   Astronomical compendium 1569 (catalogue no. 11). Reproduced by kind permission of the National Maritime Museum, London.

Plate V

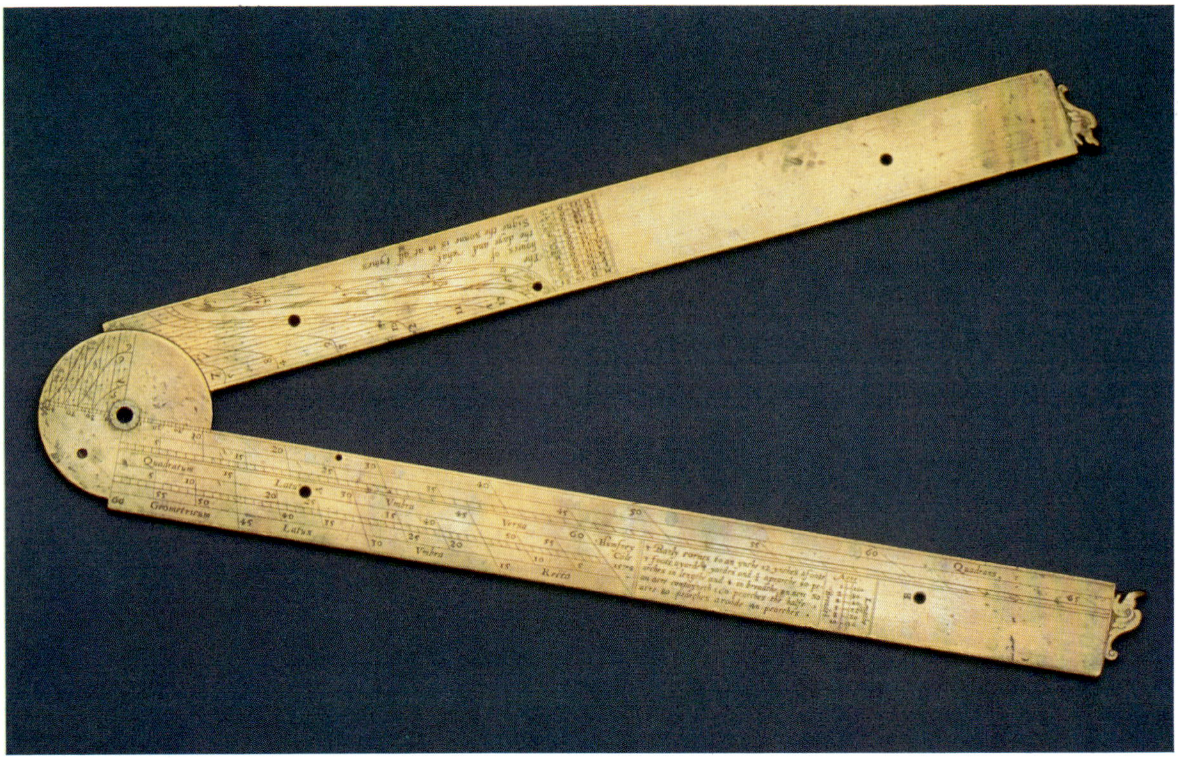

Figure 31 Folding rule 1574 (catalogue no. 18). Reproduced by kind permission of the Science & Society Picture Library.

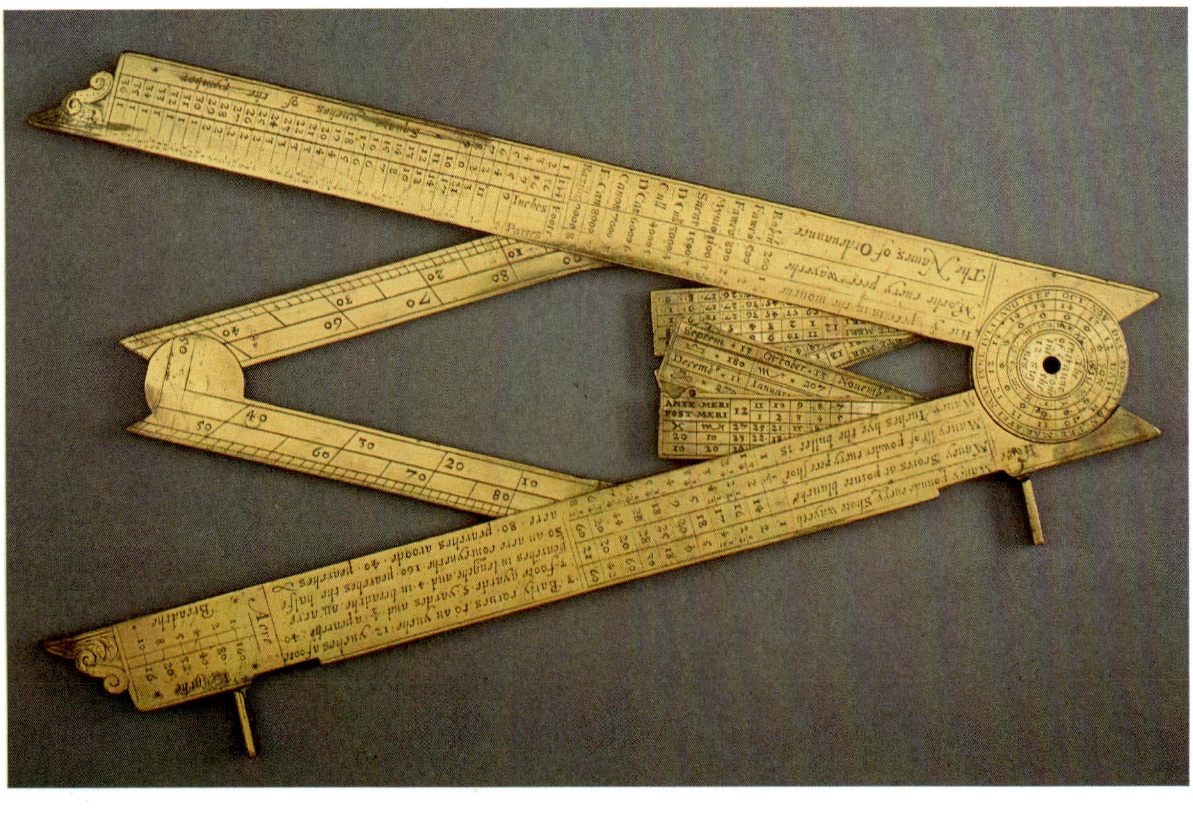

Figure 35 Folding gunner's rule 1575 (catalogue no. 21). Reproduced by kind permission of the Trustees of the British Museum

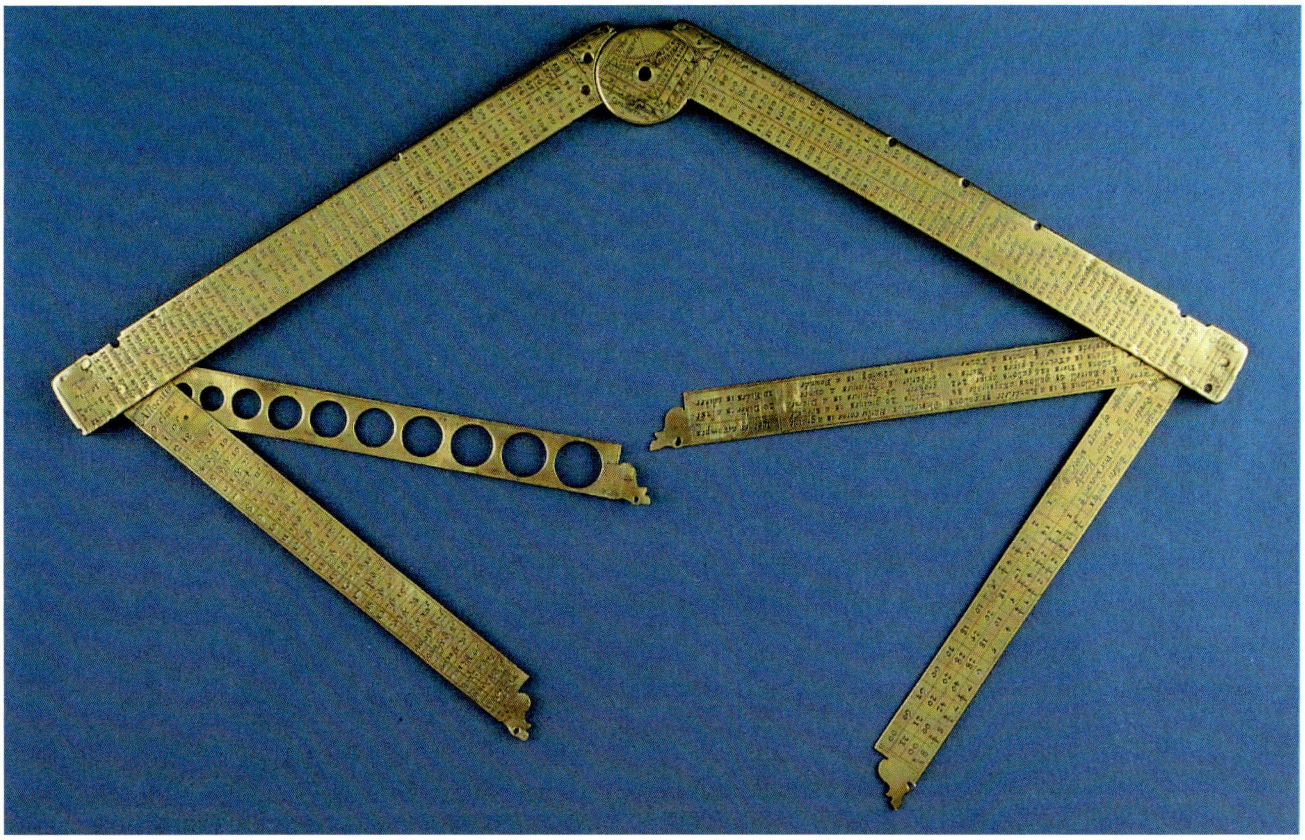

Figure 37 Folding gunner's rule (catalogue no. 23). Reproduced by kind permission of the Royal Artillery Historical Trust, Woolwich.

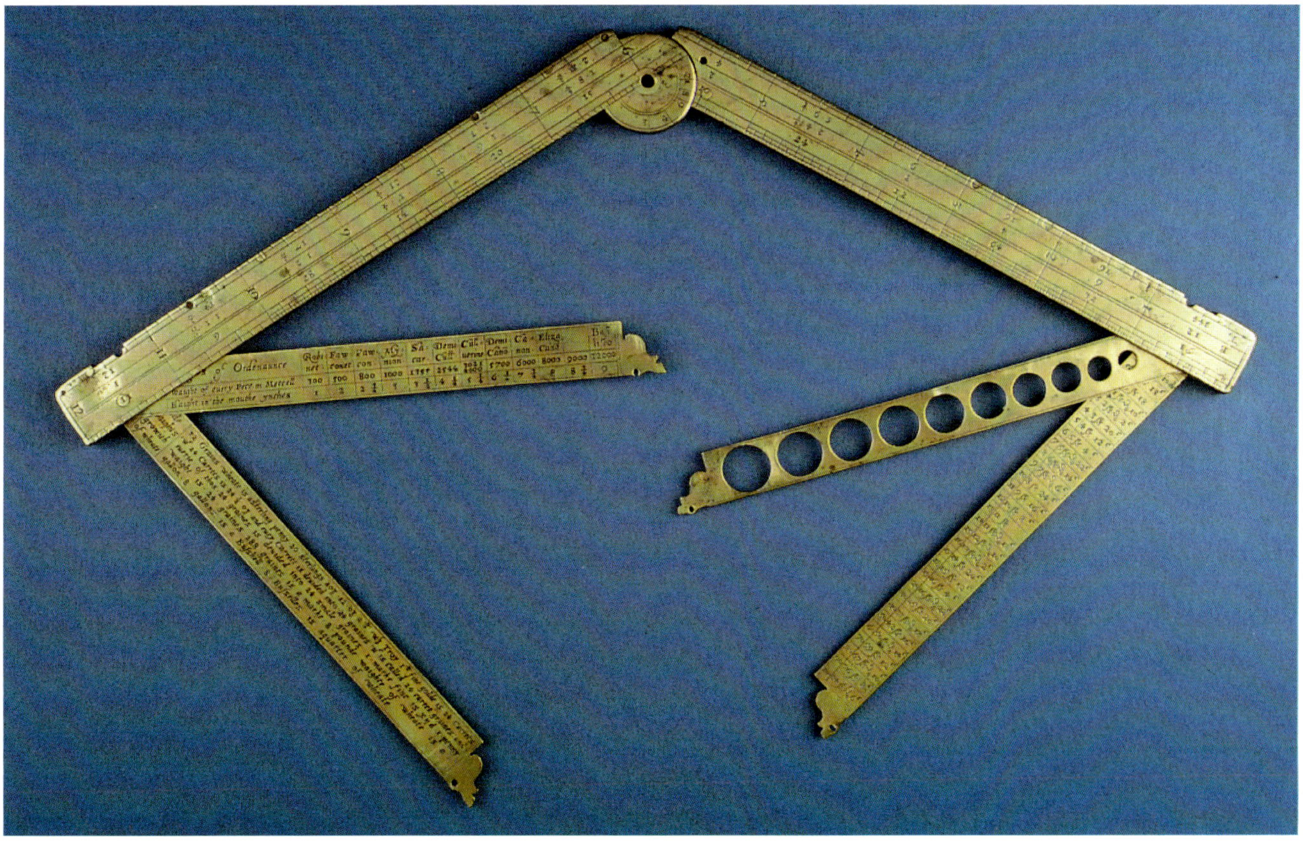

Figure 38 Folding gunner's rule (catalogue no. 23). Reproduced by kind permission of the Royal Artillery Historical Trust, Woolwich.

Astronomical Compendia

Astronomical compendia are complex pocket devices serving many purposes. Of various shapes, they contain a multitude of instruments and tables such as equatorial sundials, compasses, nocturnals, perpetual calendars, and latitude lists - sometimes even astrolabes, drawing instruments or simple theodolites.
Seven compendia made by Humphrey Cole between 1568 and 1590 have survived, five of which are very similar to each other: in a circular box they contain a nocturnal, a latitude list, a universal equatorial sundial, a compass, and a perpetual calendar (catalogue nos. 12-16). The instrument in Oxford (catalogue no. 10) is unusual in being shaped in book form and the oval dial in Greenwich (catalogue no. 11) offers the widest variety of instruments.

10 Astronomical compendium Figure 19 on Plate IV
Museum of the History of Science, Oxford
inv. no. 36,313
Signed and dated: HUMFRAY COOLE MADE THIS BOKE ANNO 1568
Gilt brass; closed box 66 x 60 x 20 mm

This elaborate instrument in the form of a book, the earliest surviving of Cole's compendia, was made for the printer Richard Jugge, as is clear from the badge on the front cover. A few years after its completion Cole engraved a map for Jugge's *Bishop's Bible* of 1572 (catalogue no. 27). This compendium includes a quadrant with folding sights, compartments for drawing instruments, a compass with a geometrical square, an equatorial dial, a list of latitudes and perpetual calendars.
As well as being in book form this compendium also has two clasps to keep it closed. Jugge's circular badge is engraved on the front cover: a tree with a bird perched on one of the upper branches. The word 'IUGGE', representing the bird's song and simultaneously the owner's name, is engraved four times in a scroll. The space around the badge is filled with animated scrollwork.
The inside of the cover is engraved with a quadrant with folding sights, named 'A quadrant to take ye hight of the so<n>ne [moon star] and ye hight of toures or any other buildi<n>ges'.
There are two different arc scales: the outer, marked 'Quadrans Astronomicus', has a degree scale 0 - 90 and 90 - 0, numbered by 10 and divided to 1. The inner scale, a 'Quadrans Geometricus' has a scale 0 - 12 - 0, numbered by 3 and divided to 3, 1 and ½. The sides of shadow square are labelled 'Vmbrae Rectae' and 'Vmbrae Versae'.
A plumb bob, necessary for using the quadrant and fitted to a projecting pin, is now missing.
The facing leaf has two compartments for drawing instruments which once contained 'THE COMPASE SQUARE & RULE' and 'THE WRYTTINGE PENNE'.
The other side of the same leaf has a circular degree scale with a geometrical square and an inset compass surrounded by a compass rose. All these elements are part of the same removable unit.
The degree scale 0 - 360 is numbered by 10 and divided to 2 by alternate shading. The square has a scale 12 - 0 - 12 on each side, numbered by 3 and divided to 1 by alternate shading. The compass rose has 31 unmarked points and north shown by a fleur-de-lis. The compass sits in a silvered bowl.
An equatorial sundial hinged to the same leaf has an hour circle mounted on a crescent-shaped support, so that it can be rotated. One side it has a 24-hour scale, numbered twice I-XII and divided to half and quarter-hours. The other side for winter use is marked for 12 hours, numbered VI - XII - VI and divided to half-hours.
Fixed to the hour ring is a skeletonised latitude quadrant with a degree scale 0 - 90 on both sides, numbered by 10 and divided to 2 and 1. The edge at 90 degrees is extended to form a pin gnomon. The latitude quadrant slides into a notch in the supporting crescent to enable the dial to be set for the appropriate latitude. A plumb bob, originally fixed to a hole in the apex of the quadrant, is now missing.
The equatorial dial can be folded into a recess in the lower leaf which is inscribed with 'THE LATITV{DES} OF PRINCIPALL TOWNES' as follows:

Lisibon	39 38
Bruxella	51
Antwerpia	51 28
Gandauum	51 24
Amsterdama	52 40
Middelburgum	51 48
Douer	51 0
Exiter	51
Oxforde	51 50
Bristowe	52
Norwiche	52 30
Leiseter	52 50
Harforde	52 50
Northampto<n>	52 50
Notingam	53
Linckole	53 15
Tolet<m>	39 56
Rone	49
Tolosa	43 30
Parisius	47 55
Monspessulanus	42 5
Marsilia	43 6
Westchester	53 10
Yorke	54
Newcastell	55
Barwicke	56 50
Edenboro	57
Dantiseum	55 0
Lubecum	54 48

Colonia	51
Francophordia	50 12
Augusta	47 32

On the other side of this leaf is a perpetual calendar comprising the first half of the year. Each day is noted with its corresponding Day Letter (1 January = A etc.), with Saints' days, Christian feasts, the dates of the sun's entry into a particular sign, and the beginnings of the seasons. The second half of the calendar is missing.

The design of the calendar follows the layout given by Leonard Digges in his *Prognostication* of 1555 (Figure 20).

The following dates are listed (only those entries are given here which contain more than just the Day Letter. The symbols for the sun and the zodiacal signs are expressed here in words):

Januar

1 A	Circu
6 e	Epiph
11 d	sun in Aquarius
13 f	Hilar
25 d	Pau

Februa

2 e	Puri
9 e	sun in Pisces
14 c	Valent
24 f	Mat

March

11 g	sun in Aries
12 A	Spri<n>g
25 g	Annu

Aprill

4 d	Ambro
11 c	sun in Taurus
23 A	Georg
25 c	Marc

Maye

1 b	Phi Iac
6 g	Io Eua
10 d	Io
12 f	sun in Gemini
26 f	Augus

Iune

11 A	Barna
12 b	sun in Cancer
13 c	Su<m>mer
24 g	Ioa bap
29 e	Pe Pa

Bibliography

Gunther, R.T., 'The Great Astrolabe and other Scientific Instruments of Humphrey Cole', *Archaeologia* 76 (1927), pp. 273-317, esp. 281-285.

11 Astronomical compendium Figure 21 on Plate IV
National Maritime Museum, Greenwich
inv. no. AST0172 (previously D.318)
Signed and dated twice:
Humfray Colle made this diall anno 1569
HC 1569
Gilt brass; closed oval box 82 x 57 x 23 mm.

This astronomical compendium is the most elaborate instrument in the group described.

It includes a lunar volvelle, a perpetual calendar, a list of latitudes, a universal equatorial dial, a compass, a simple theodolite, and an instrument for calculating the time of high tide at various listed ports and harbours.

Like all the other compendia by Cole this instrument is fitted with a suspension apparatus which allows it to be suspended from a belt or probably to be worn on a chain around the owner's neck.

The back and cover of the oval case both show an engraved scene. Both engravings are taken from designs by Etienne Delaune (1518-1583 or 1595) and represent Juno and Jupiter.

The inside of the cover contains a lunar volvelle consisting of an engraved plate and two movable discs each with an index.

The plate is inscribed with two circular scales: a Julian calendar with the ususal Latin names of the months and the corresponding number of days (numbered by 10 and divided to 2); and a scale marked with the usual Latin names of the zodiacal signs (each with a 30° scale, numbered by 10 and divided to 2).

The larger disc with an index with a sun effigy, is marked 'The course of the Sonne and Mone throughe 12 Signes'. It shows the age of the moon 1 - 29½, numbered by 1 and divided to ¼.

The smaller disc with a small index is marked with an aspectarium. A circular aperture shows the phases of the moon.

The facing leaf with perpetual calendar, is inscribed in the centre 'A kalender with ye Saint<s> daies and moueable feastes for euer'.

The three outer circles give the dates of Saints' days and Christian feasts as well as the date of the sun's entry into a particular sign, the seasons and seasonal events such as the Dog days. They are arranged vertically in four sections, i.e. January, February and March are in the first, starting with January at the top etc.

The following dates can be read off:

January

1	Circu
6	Epiph
11	sun in Aquarius
13	Hilar
25	Co P

Februa

2	Purifi
10	sun in Pisces

A general

The first part of the generall Kalendar: from Ianuarie to Iune.

Ianuarie.	Februarie	March.	Dayes	April.	May.	Iune.
:A Circūc.	d	d	1	g	b Ph.Iac.	e
:b	e Purifi.	e	2	A	c	f
c	f	f	3	b	.d	g
:d	g	g	4	c	e	:A
:e	A	A	5	d	f	b
f Epiph.	b	b	6	e	.g	c
g	c	c	7	.f	:d	:d
A	:d	d.	8	.g	b	e
b	e ☉ in ♓	e	9	A	c	f
:c ☉ in ♒	:f	f	10	.b	d	.g
d	g	g ☉ in ♈	11	c ☉ in ♉	e	A Barna.
e	A	A	12	d	f ☉ in ♊	b ☉ in ♋
f Hilar.	b	b	13	e	g	c
g	c Valent.	c	14	f	A	d
:A	d	:d	15	g	:b	.e
b	e	:e	16	:A	c	f
:c	:f	f	17	b	d	g
d	g	g	18	c	e	A
e	A	:A	19	d	f	b
f	b	b	20	.e	:g	c
g	c	c	21	:f	A	d
A	d	d	22	g	b	.e
b	e	e	23	A Georg.	c	f
c	f Mat.	f	24	b	d	g Ioā bap.
d Cō.Pau.	g	g Annun.	25	c Marc.	e	A
e	.A	A	26	d	f	b
f	.b	b	27	e	g	c
g	.c	.c	28	f	A	d
:A		d	29	g	b.	e Pe.Pa.
b		e	30	A	c	f
c		f	31		d	

Figure 20 'A general calendar', Leonard Digges, Prognostication, *printed by Thomas Gemini London 1555 (British Library 718.g.5). Reproduced by kind permission of the British Library.*

14	Valen
24	Matt

March

11	sun in Aries
12	Spring
25	Anunci

April

11	sun in Taurus
23	George
25	Marcke

May

1	Phillip Iacob
12	sun in Gemini

June

11	Barna
12	sun in Cancer
24	Io ba
29	Pe

July

6	Dog beg (the beginning of the dog days)
14	sun in Taurus
22	Ma ma
25	Ia Apo

August

1	Pe Vi
14	sun in Virgo
17	Do en (the end of the dog days)
24	Ba

September

8	Na Ma
14	sun in Libra
21	Mat
29	Mi

October

14	sun in Scorpio
18	Luke
28	Simon Iude

November

1	Om Sa
2	Om An
13	sun in Sagittarius
30	Andr

December

6	Ni
8	Co m
12	sun in Capricorn
21	Tho A
25	Na

The five circles in the middle give a table with the dates of Easter Day ('East D'), Day Letters of those days ('Do Le'), the Golden Numbers ('Prime'), and the Dominical Letters for ordinary years and leap years ('Do L' and 'Le y').
The table starts with 21 March corresponding to Golden Number 18 and the Dominical Letter B, and ends with 25 April with the Day Letter C.
The two circles in the centre are marked with tables for the Golden Numbers ('Pri') and the corresponding Epacts (marked 'Epact') as follows, starting with 12 / 12 and ending with 11 /1.
The instrument is signed and dated 'HC 1560' in the centre of the calendar.
The other side of the above leaf contains a list of latitudes as follows:

Douer	51
Exiter	51
London	51 34
Norwiche	52 30
Oxforde	51 50
Leiseter	52 50
Harforde	52 50
Bristowe	52 0
Northamto<n>	52 50
W·chestr	53 10
Linckolne	53 15
Notingam	53 0
Yorke	54 0
Newecaste	55 0
Barwic	56 50
Edenbo	57
Saulis	51 34
Cambrig	52 0
Baseingsto	51 34
Paris	47 55
Antwerp	51 28
Colonia	51 0
Venetia	44 50
Basileia	48 0
Compostellae	44 20
Augusta	48 0
Lisbona	39 0
Neapoli	39 0
Lions	45 0
Rouan	48 0
Toledo	39 0
Roma	42

A universal equatorial sundial is hinged between this and the lower leaf.
The hour circle is mounted on a crescent-shaped support, so that it can be rotated. One side is marked with a 24-hour scale, numbered twice I-XII and divided to half-hours. The other side for use in winter is marked for 12 hours, numbered VI - XII - VI and divided to half-hours.
The signature of the maker and the date 'Humfrey Côle 1575' are engraved on this side of the hour ring.

Fixed to the hour ring is a skeletonised latitude quadrant with a degree scale 0 - 90, numbered by 10 and divided to 2. The other side, for use in winter, is marked for 12 hours, numbered VI - XII - VI and divided to half-hours. The edge at 90° is extended to form a pin gnomon. The latitude quadrant slides into a notch in the supporting crescent which enables the dial to be set for the appropriate latitude. A plumb bob originally fixed to a hole in the apex of the quadrant is now missing.
The facing side of the fourth leaf is laid out as a simple theodolite, consisting of a degree scale 0 - 360 (numbered by 10 and divided to 2), an inset 'Geometricall Square' with a scale 12 - 0 - 12 on each side (numbered by 3 and divided to 1) and a compass in the centre. The latter indicates the eight main points with a fleur-de-lis for north. An engraved ring around the compass indicates 32 compass directions. The alidade with folding sights is held by a ring around the compass.
The other side of this leaf has a list of ports and harbours grouped by compass directions. It is titled 'THE NAMES PRI<N>CIPAL PORTES & HAVENS OF VROPE WHAT MONE MAKETH AFVLL SEA'. These are as follows

S
Spetes
Shew
Quin
Southeha<m>to<n>
Porch¯

SBW
ye west end of ye nore
Redbã
Aberdē
3 Illa<n>d<s>

SSW
Do˜ber in Scot
Coding
Rode
Barwic
Holy Iland & So to
Tinmot
Cro Ila

SWBS
Burli<n>gt in the Baye
Ede<n>bor or leth in Scot
Dundee
S Andr
Graues end

SW
Londo<n>
From tinmōt to. flā borow head
Hartil
Pasag
Bilban
Alardeo

SW
Foxnoze
Riuer
Cowlai
Staples sai<n>t se bastia
S Andr
Growh
Monge
Mors

WSW
Dartmo
Plimōt
Faumo
Scilli
Milfor hauen

WBS
Toua

E
ye well

EBS
Bristo

ESE
Saint Georg<s> Iland<s>

SEBE
At Alde and at Saine head & alo<n>g ye coas of norma<n>di
Portlā

SE
Laisto
Roade
Harwi
All ye coast fr^{o} wītertū to yerm ye land<s> end

SEBE
Stand which
Douer
Rie
Deipe
Newe hauen
Lux
Lewys

SSE
Orfor
Orwell
Wand<s>
Marget
Bul
Callins

SBE
Colne
Ila<n>ds of Triost

WSW
La<n>d<s> end at ye Gulf

WSW
ye coas of Irel fro wa terfor to ki<n>g

WNW
Colue

The inside of the last leaf is laid out as an instrument for finding the times of high water, marked on the outside scales 'AN INSTRUMEN TO KNOWE THE EBBES AND FLVDDES'. It consists of three scales and two volvelles, each with an index.

The scales are inscribed as follows (from the outside):

a) a degree scale 0 - 360, numbered by 10 and divided to 2;

b) an hour ring, numbered clockwise twice I - XII;

c) a compass rose indicating 32 points by their first letters.

The larger disc, with a small pointer, is inscribed with the age of the moon 1 - 30, divided to quarter-days.

The smaller disc, with a long pointer with a lunar crescent at the end, has a circular aperture which shows the phases of the moon.

Bibliography

Gunther, R.T., 'The Great Astrolabe and other Scientific Instruments of Humphrey Cole', *Archaeologia* 76 (1927), pp. 273-317, esp. 281-285, with figs. 22-30 on pls LXIX and LXX.

12 Astronomical compendium Figure 22
British Museum, London

inv. no. MLA 1888,12-1.293
Signed and dated: Humfrey Côle 1575
Gilt brass; closed box 55 x 23 mm

This circular instrument, which is very similar to the compendium in Edinburgh dating from the same year (catalogue no. 13), consists of a nocturnal, a latitude list, a universal equatorial sundial, a compass and a perpetual calendar with Saints' days, Dominical Letters, Golden Numbers and Epacts.

The instrument has a suspension ring which allowed it to be attached to a belt or to be worn on a chain around the owner's neck.

The outside of the top leaf is laid out as a nocturnal consisting of two circular scales and two volvelles one of which has an index.

The outside scale is marked with the usual Latin names (some abbreviated) of the zodiacal signs (numbered from 1 - 12 beginning with Aries) and their symbols. Each sign has a 30 degree scale, numbered by 10 and divided to 2 by alternate shading.

The inner scale is marked with the usual Latin names of the months and the corresponding number of days, numbered by 10 and divided to 2 by alternate shading. The top centre of the instrument corresponds to *c.* 18 April. The equinoxes correspond to 11 March and 14 September, the solstices to 12 June and 12 December.

The outer volvelle, labelled 'The nighte houres', has an hour scale marked anticlockwise 4 - 12 - 9. The hours are further indicated by small teeth, an index for 12 o'clock is decorated with a sun effigy.

The central disc is marked 'THE POLE STERRE'. The index for alignment with the pole star is decorated with a moon effigy. The area around the central hole is decorated with a sun burst.

The inside of the upper leaf is marked with a list of latitudes in five concentric rings with eight entries each; a sixth central ring is inscribed 'The latitudes of all the principall townes and cities of evrope'.

The following towns are named:

Edenboro	57 0
Co<m>postel	44 20
Lisbonª	39 38
Barsalº	41 35
Na<n>tes	48 12
Parisius	47 55
Marsilia	43 6
Tolosa	43 30
Louani	50 58
Rone	49 0
Antwerpia	51 28
Bruxella	51 0
Brugae	51 30
Gandā	51 24
Tor¯a¯c	51 40
Francopho	50 12
Cracouia	51 0
Dantis¯c	55 0
Lubecu<m>	54 48
Emde<n>	53 42
Constanti	43 0
Florentia	43 4
Neapolis	41 0
Venetia	44 50
Roma	41 50
Douer	51 0
Exiter	51 0
London	51 34
Oxford	51 50
Bristo	51 0
Northampt	52 50
Norwiche	52 30
Harford	52 50
Leisetr	52 50
Noting	53 0
W Chester	53 10
Linckoll	53 15
Yorke	54 0
N cast	55 0
Barwic	56 50

A universal equatorial sundial is hinged between the upper and lower leaf of the compendium.

The hour circle is mounted on a crescent-shaped support, so that it can be rotated. One side is marked with a

Figure 22 Astronomical compendium 1575 (catalogue no. 12). Reproduced by kind permission of the Trustees of the British Museum.

24-hour scale, numbered twice I-XII and divided to half-hours. The other side for use in winter is marked for 12 hours, numbered VI - XII - VI and divided to half-hours. The signature of the maker and the date 'Humfrey Côle 1575' are engraved on this side of the hour ring.
Fixed to the hour ring is a skeletonised latitude quadrant with a degree scale 0 - 90, numbered by 10 and divided to 2. The edge at 90° is extended to form a pin gnomon. The latitude quadrant slides in a notch in the supporting crescent which enables the dial to be set for the appropriate latitude. A plumb bob originally fixed in a hole in the apex of the quadrant is now missing.
A magnetic compass with a painted compass card in gold, green, grey and burgundy is set into the inside of the lower leaf. Thirty-two points are indicated with the eight main points marked in full, the others marked with their first letters 'NORTH, NBE, NNE, NEBN, NORTH EAST, NEBE, ENE, EBN' etc. North is further indicated by a fleur-de-lis, east by a cross, south by an arrow and west by a spade.
The outside of the lower leaf is laid out as a perpetual calendar with Saints' days, Christian feasts, Dominical Letters, Golden Numbers and Epacts, consisting of seven circles and titled in the centre 'THIS TABLE BEGIN<N>ETH AT 1572 & SO FOR EVER'.
The three outer circles give the dates of 38 Saints' days and Christian feasts. The following dates are given:

I	1 Circū	6 Epiph	13 Hill	25 Co Pau
F	2 Puri Ma	16 Valē	25 Mat Ap	
M	12 Grego	25 Annū Ma		
A	4 Ambro	23 George	25 Marcus	
M	1 Phi Iac	6 Iō Evā	26 Augus	
I	11 Barn	24 Iō Ba	29 Pe Pa	
I	2 Visi Ma	22 Ma Mag	23 Iā Ap	
A	1 Pi Vi	10 Lau	24 Bar	29 De Io
S	8 Nat Ma	21 Mar	29 Mic	
O	13 Edwa Cꝰō	18 Lu	28 Sī ·Iude	
N	1 Om Sā	2 Om Anī	30 Andr	
D	6 Ni	8 Cꝰō	21 Thō	25 Na

The two circles in the middle give a list of Dominical Letters for ordinary years and leap years ('DO LE' and 'LE Y') starting with F/E and running clockwise to G.
The two circles in the centre are marked with tables for the Golden Numbers ('PRI') and the corresponding Epacts ('EPA') as follows:

15	15	
16	26	
17	7	
18	18	
19	29	(recte 0)
1	11	
2	22	
3	3	
4	14	
5	25	
6	6	
7	17	
8	28	
9	9	
10	20	
11	1	
12	12	
13	23	(recte 23)
14	4	

The outer rim is engraved as follows:
'AS TIME AND HOVRES PASITH AWAYE SO DOETH THE LIFE OF MAN DECAY' and 'AS TIME CAN BE REDEMED WITH NO COST BESTOW IT WELL AND LET NO HOWR BE LOST'.
The rim is decorated with a rope-twist design.
The suspension consists of a sphere supported by two scrolls with an inset ring through which passes a loose ring.
The instrument retains its original fitted brown-leather case stamped in gold and lined with red velvet.

Bibliography

Gunther, R.T., 'The Great Astrolabe and Other Scientific Instruments of Humphrey Cole', *Archaeologia* 76 (1927), pp. 289-291 and figs 34-35.

Ward, F.A.B., *A Catalogue of European Scientific Instruments in the Department of Medieval and Later Antiquities of the British Museum* (London 1981), pp. 125 ff., no. 360.

13 Astronomical compendium — Figure 23
National Museums of Scotland, Edinburgh

inv. no. NL 18
Signed and dated: Humfrey Côle 1575
Gilt brass; closed box 54 x 20 mm

This instrument is very similar to the compendium in the British Museum (catalogue no. 12). It consists of a nocturnal, a latitude list, an equatorial sundial, a compass and a perpetual calendar with the names of Saints, Dominical Letters, Golden Numbers and Epacts.
The instrument has a suspension ring which allowed it to be attached to a belt or to be worn on a chain around the owner's neck.
The outside on the top leaf is laid out as a nocturnal consisting of two circular scales and two volvelles one of which has an index.
The outside scale is marked with the usual Latin names (some abbreviated) of the zodiacal signs (numbered from 1 to 12 beginning with Aries) and their symbols. Each sign has a 30 degree scale, numbered by 10 and divided to 2 by alternate shading.
The inner scale is marked with the usual Latin names of the months and the corresponding number of days, numbered by 10 and divided to 2 by alternate shading. The top centre of the instrument corresponds to *c.* 18 April. The equinoxes correspond to 11 March and 14 September, the solstices to 12 June and 12 December.
The central disc is marked 'THE POLE STERRE', but the index for alignment with the polar star is broken off. The area around the central hole is decorated with a sun burst.

Figure 23 *Astronomical compendium 1575 (catalogue no. 13). Reproduced by kind permission of the Trustees of the National Museums of Scotland.*

The inside of the upper leaf is marked with a list of latitudes in five concentric rings with eight entries each; a sixth central ring is inscribed 'The latitudes of all the principall townes and cities of evrope'.
The following towns are named:

Edenboro	57 0
Co<m>postell	44 20
Lisbona	39 38
Barsalo	41 35
Nante<s>	48 12
Parisius	47 55
Marsilia	43 6
Tolosa	43 30
Louani	50 58
Rone	49 0
Antwerpia	51 28
Bruxella	51 0
Brugae	51 30
Ganda¯u	51 24
Torna¯c	51 40
Francopho	50 12
Cracouia	51 0
Dantis¯c	55 0
Lubecu<m>	54 48
Emde<n>	53 42
Constanti	43 0
Florentia	43 4
Neapolis	41 0
Venetia	44 50
Roma	41 50
Douer	51 0
Exiter	51 0
London	51 34
Oxford	51 50
Bristo	51 0
Northamp	52 50
Norwiche	52 30
Harford	52 50
Leiset<er>	52 50
Noting	53 0
W·chester	53 10
Linckoll	53 15
Yorke	54 0
N·cast	55 0
Barwic	56 50

A universal equatorial sundial is hinged between the upper and lower leaf of the compendium.
The hour circle is mounted on a crescent-shaped support, so that it can be rotated. One side is marked with a 24-hour scale, numbered twice I-XII and divided to half-hours.
The other side for use in winter is marked for 12 hours, numbered VI - XII - VI and divided to half-hours.
The signature of the maker and the date 'Humfrey Côle 1575' are engraved on this side of the hour ring.
Fixed to the hour ring is a skeletonised latitude quadrant with a degree scale 0 - 90, numbered by 10 and divided to 2. The edge at 90° is extended to form a pin gnomon. The latitude quadrant slides in a notch in the supporting crescent which enables the dial to be set for the appropriate latitude. A plumb bob originally fixed in a hole in the apex of the quadrant is now missing.
A magnetic compass with a painted compass card in gold, green, grey and burgundy is set in the inside of the lower leaf. Thirty-two points are indicated with the eight main points marked in full, the others marked with their first letters 'NORTH, NBE, NNE, NEBN, NORTH EAST, NEBE, ENE, EBN' etc. North is further indicated by a fleur-de-lis, east by a cross, south by an arrow and west by a spade.
The edge of the card is marked with a 360 degree scale, numbered by 10.
The outside of the lower leaf is laid out as a perpetual calendar with Saints' days, Christian feasts, Dominical Letters, Golden Numbers and Epacts, consisting of seven circles and titled in the centre 'THIS TABLE BEGINNETH AT 1572 AND SO FOR EVER.
The three outer circles give the dates of 38 Saints' days and Christian feasts. The following dates are given:

I	1 Circū	6 Epiph	13 Hill	25 C'Pau
F	2 Puri Ma	16 Valē	25 Mat Ap	
M	12 Grego	25 Annū Ma		
A	4 Ambro	23 George	25 Marcus	
M	1 Phi Iac	6 Iō Evā	26 Augus	
I	11 Barn	24 Iō Ba	29 Pe Pa	
I	2 Visi Ma	22 Ma Mag	23 Iā Ap	
A	1 Pi Vi	10 Lau	24 Bar	29 De Io
S	8 Nat Ma	21 Mar	29 Mic	
O	13 Edwa C^{9}ō	18 Lu	28 Sim Iude	
N	1 Om Sā	2 Om Anī	30 Andr	
D	6 Ni	8 C^{9}ō	21 Thō	25 Na

The two circles in the middle give a list of Dominical Letters for ordinary years and leap years (marked 'DO LE' and 'LE Y') starting with F/E and running clockwise to G.
The two circles in the centre are marked with tables for the Golden Numbers (marked 'PRIM') and the corresponding Epacts (marked 'EPA') as follows:

15	15	
16	26	
17	7	
18	18	
19	29	(recte 0)
1	11	
2	22	
3	3	
4	14	
5	25	

6	6	
7	17	
8	28	
9	9	
10	20	
11	1	
12	12	
13	13	(recte 23)
14	4	

The outer rim is engraved as follows:
'AS TIME AND HOVRES PASITH AWAYE SO DOETH THE LIFE OF MAN DECAYE (corrected from DDCAVE)
AS TIME CAN BE REDEMED WITH NO COST BESTOW IT WELL AND LET NO HOWR BE LOST'.
The rim is decorated with a rope-twist design.
The suspension consists of a sphere supported by two scrolls with an inset ring through wich passes a loose ring.

Bibliography

Gunther, R.T., 'The Great Astrolabe and Other Scientific Instruments of Humphrey Cole', *Archaeologia* 76 (1927), pp. 289-291 and fig. 33.

14 Astronomical compendium — Figure 24 on Plate I
Signed and dated: Humfrey Côle 1579 — Figure 25

Gilt brass; closed box 55 x 20 mm
Private Collection

This compendium of 1579, now in a private collection, closely resembles the instrument in Liège of the same date (catalogue no. 15), although the latter has several replacements.
The instrument consists of a perpetual calendar, a compass, an equatorial sundial, a list of latitudes, a nocturnal, a table of the entry of the sun into a particular zodiacal sign (the instrument in Liège has a table of the ruling planets of the hours instead), a shadow square, a diagram for unequal hours and an alidade.
The outside of the lid is inscribed with a perpetual calendar consisting of seven circles. The centre is labelled 'THIS TABLE BEGINITH AT A 1579 AN SO FOR EVER'.
The three outer circles give the dates of 36 Saints' days and Christian feasts. The following dates are given:

I	1 Circũ	6 Epiph	13 Hill	25 Con Pau
F	2 Puri Ma	16 Vali	25 Mat Apo	
M	12 Grigo	25 Annũ Mary		
A	4 Ambro	23 George	25 Marcus	
M	1 Phi Iac	6 Iõ Evã	26 Augus	
I	11 Barn	24 Iõ Ba	29 Pe Pa	
I	2 Visi Ma	22 Ma Mag	25 Iã Apo	
A	1 Pe Vin	24 Barth	29 Dec Ione	
S	8 Nat Ma	21 Mar	29 Mich	
O	18 Lucke Evã	28 Simon Iude		
N	1 Al Saintes	30 Andro Apos		
D	6 Ni	8 Cõma	21 Thõ ap	25 Na

The two circles in the middle give a list of Dominical Letters for ordinary years and leap years (marked 'DOMI L' and 'LEP Y') starting with D and clockwise running to E.
The two circles in the centre are marked with tables for the Golden Numbers (marked 'PRIM') and the corresponding Epacts (marked 'EPAC') as follows:

3	3	
4	14	
5	25	
6	6	
7	17	
8	28	
9	9	
10	20	
11	1	
12	12	
13	23	
14	4	
15	15	
16	26	
17	7	
18	18	
19	29	(recte 0)
1	11	
2	22	

A magnetic compass with a painted compass card in white, green, and burgundy on a terracotta background is set into the inside of the upper leaf. Thirty-two points are indicated with the eight main points marked in full, the others marked with their first letters 'NORTH, NBE, NNE, NEBN, NORTH EAST, NEBE, ENE, EBN' etc. North is marked with a fleur-de-lis, east with a cross, south with an arrow and west with a spade. The compass needle and glass are replacements.
A universal equatorial sundial is attached to the same hinge as the lid.
The hour circle is mounted on a crescent-shaped support, so that it can be rotated. One side is marked with a 24-hour scale, numbered twice I - XII and divided to half-hours by alternate shading. The other side for use in winter is marked for 12 hours, numbered VI - XII - VI and divided to half-hours by alternate shading.
The signature of the maker and the date 'Humfrey Côle 1579' are inscribed on this side of the hour ring.
Fixed to the hour ring is a skeletonised latitude quadrant with a degree scale 0 - 90, numbered by 10 and divided to 2. The edge at 90° is extended to form a pin gnomon. The latitude quadrant slides in a notch in the supporting crescent which enables the dial to be set for the appropriate latitude. A plumb bob originally fixed in a hole in the apex of the quadrant is now missing.
The inside of the base of the compendium is inscribed with a list of 32 latitudes consisting of four circles with eight entries each; a fifth central circle is marked 'The names of sites and townes of vrope'.

The following towns are named:

Douer	51 0
Exiter	51 0
Londō	51 30
Oxfor	51 50
Norwiche	52 30
Harforde	52 50
Lesetur	52 50
Bristo	52 0
Norhamtū	52 50
Notingā	53 0
W·chestr	53 10
Lincon	53 15
Nucastell	55 0
Barwick	56 50
Edenbor	57 0
Yorke	54 0
Composte	44 20
Lisbona	39 38
Barsal	41 35
Rone	49 0
Parisius	47 55
Marsili	43 6
Louani	50 58
Tolosa	43 30
Anwarpe	51 28
Bruge	51 30
Cracoui	51 0
Praga	50 4
Dantis	55 0
Emdem	53 42
Veniti	44 50
Colon	51 0

Hinged to this part of the compendium with the latitude list is a plate which is engraved on one side with a table of the dates of the sun's entry into a particular sign (A), and on the other side as a nocturnal (B).

A) The table is marked in the centre 'A table for the son<n>es entraun in to anye the 12 signes'. The signature of the maker 'H Côle' is repeated here.

The table is laid out in four circular scales as follows (from the outside): the first letter of each month, the date of the sun's entry, the effigy of the sun 12 times, the signs indicated by their symbols. The following dates can be read off:

11 January	Aquarius
10 February	Pisces
11 March	Aries
11 April	Taurus
12 May	Gemini
12 June	Cancer
14 July	Leo
14 August	Virgo
14 September	Libra
14 October	Scorpio
13 November	Sagittarius
12 December	Capricorn

B) The nocturnal consists of two circular scales and two volvelles, each with an index.

The outside scale is marked anticlockwise with the names of the months in English as follows: 'Ianiary, Februa, March, Aprill, Maye, Iune, Iulye, August, Septem, October, Nouem, Decemb'. Each month is marked with the corresponding number of days (December has 31.25 days to indicate the leap year), numbered by 10 and divided to 2. The top centre of the instrument corresponds to *c.* 18 April.

The outer volvelle has a 24-hour scale marked anticlockwise twice 1 - 12. The hours are further indicated by small teeth, 12 o'clock with an index.

The central disc is marked 'The pole star' and has an 'INDEX POLARIS'. The area around the central hole is decorated with a sun burst.

The outisde of the lid is engraved with a degree scale 0 - 90 - 0 - 90 - 0, starting at the east-west line, numbered by 10 and divided to 2.

In the top half of the vacant space is a double horary quadrant for unequal hours, numbered 1 - 6 - 12 and marked 'Hora planetaru<m>'.

The lower half is inscribed with a double shadow scale to the base 12, marked 'Vmbra Versa' and 'Vmbra Recta', numbered by 3 and divided to 1.

A counterchanged alidade, with the sighting vanes missing, rotates over this face.

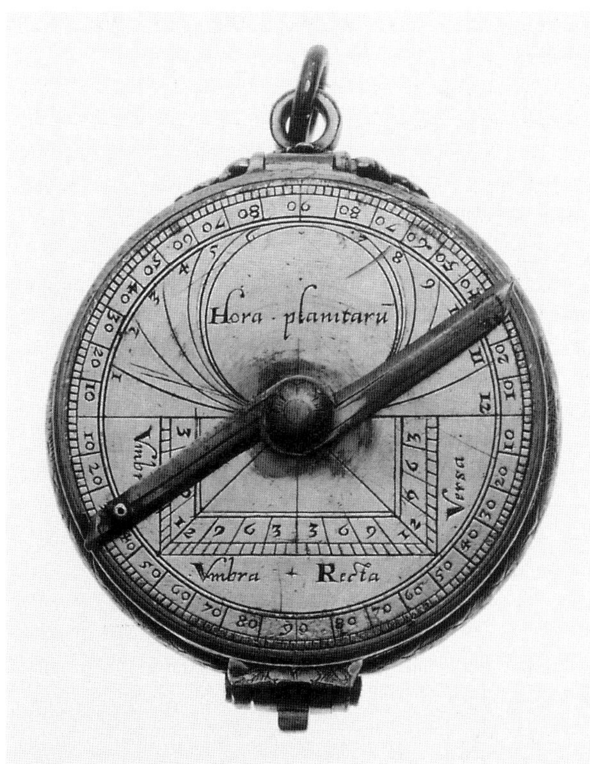

Figure 25 Astronomical compendium 1579 (catalogue no. 14). Reproduced by kind permission of Christie's, London.

The outer edge of the instrument is inscribed with a motto which may come either from Harrison's *Description of Britain* of 1577, III, 3, p. 99, or John Owen, *Epigrams*, *c.* 1560-1622: 'TEMPORA MVTANTVR & NOS MVTAMVR IN ILLIS' (i.e. Times change and we change with them) and a quotation from I Chronicles 29,15 'SICVT VMBRA DIES NOSTRI SVPER TERRAM' (i.e. Our days on Earth are as a shadow).
The instrument is fitted with a suspension ring which allowed it to be suspended from a belt or perhaps to be worn on a chain around the owner's neck.

Bibliography

Christie's South Kensington, London Sale Catalogue, 29 March 1990, lot 231.

Time. Catalogue of an exhibition in Amsterdam 1990, ed. A.J. Turner, (The Hague 1990), no. 230, pp. 117 f.

Turner, Gerard L'E., 'Misurazione del Tempo', in *Gli Strumenti*, (Milan 1990), pp. 126-127.

15 Astronomical Compendium — Figure 26
Musée de la Vie Wallonne, Liège

inv. no. 505
Signed and dated: Humfrey Côle 1579
Gilt brass; closed box 55 x 27 mm

This circular instrument is very similar to the compendium in a private collection (catalogue no. 14), but has several replacement parts. It consists of a perpetual calendar, a universal equatorial sundial, a list of latitudes, a nocturnal, a table of the planetary rulers of the hours (catalogue no. 14 has a table of the entry of the sun into a particular zodiacal sign instead), a shadow square, a diagram for unequal hours and an alidade. The outside of the lid is inscribed with a perpetual calendar consisting of seven circles. The centre is marked 'THIS BEGINES AT A 1579 & SO FOR EVER'.
The three outer circles give the dates of 36 Saints' days and Christian feasts. The following dates are given:

I	1 Circū	6 Epiph	13 Hill	25 Cōpa
F	2 Pur Ma	14 Valē	24 Ma ap	
M	12 Grigo	25 Anū Ma		
A	4 Ambro	23 Georg	25 Marcu'	
M	1 Phi Iac	6 Iō evā	26 Augus	
I	11 Bar	24 Iō ba	29 Pe Pa	
I	2 Visi Ma	22 Ma Mag	25 Iac Apo	
A	1 Pe Vin	24 Bart	29 De Iō	
S	8 Na Ma	21 Mar	29 Mi	
O	13 Edwa	18 Luc	28 Simō Iud	
N	1 Om sa	2 Om an	30 Andr	
D	8 Cōma	21 Thō ap	25 Nat	

The two circles in the middle give a list of Dominical Letters for ordinary years and leap years (marked 'Do Le' and 'Lep Y') starting with D and running clockwise to E.
The two circles in the centre are marked with tables for the Golden Numbers (marked 'Pri') and the corresponding Epacts (marked 'Epa') as follows:

3	3	
4	14	
5	25	
6	6	
7	17	
8	28	
9	9	
10	20	
11	1	
12	12	
13	23	
14	4	
15	15	
16	26	
17	7	
18	18	
19	29	(recte 0)
1	11	
2	22	

A magnetic compass is missing, and the space is filled with a metal plate with engraving similar to that on the outside, but much cruder in execution.
A universal equatorial sundial is attached to the same hinge as the lid.
The hour circle is mounted on a crescent-shaped support, so that it can be rotated. One side is marked with a 24-hour scale, numbered twice I - XII and divided to half-hours by alternate shading. The other side for use in winter is marked for 12 hours, numbered VI - XII - VI and divided to half-hours by alternate shading. The signature of the maker and the date 'Humfrey Côle 1579' are inscribed on this side of the hour ring.
Fixed to the hour ring is a skeletonised latitude quadrant with a degree scale 0 - 90, numbered by 10 and divided to 2. The edge at 90° is extended to form a pin gnomon. The latitude quadrant slides in a notch in the supporting crescent which enables the dial to be set for the appropriate latitude. A plumb bob originally fixed in a hole in the apex of the quadrant is now missing.
The inside of the base of the compendium is inscribed with a list of 32 latitudes consisting of four circles with eight entries each; a fifth central circle is labelled 'The names of sites and tounes of vrope'. An index fixed in the centre rotates over the whole radius.
The following towns are named:

Londo<n>	51 34
Exiter	51 0
Douer	51 0
Oxfo	51 50
Norwich	52 30
Harfor	52 50
Leset	52 50
Bris	52 0
Norhātū	52 50
Noting	53 0

Figure 26 Astronomical compendium 1579 (catalogue no. 15). Reproduced by kind permission of the Musée de la Vie Wallonne, Liège.

W·ches	53 10
Lincō	53 15
N·castell	55 0
Barwic	56 50
Ede<n>bor	57 0
York	54 0
Cōposte	44 20
Lisbōa	39 38
Brsalo	41 35
Rone	49 0
Parisius	47 55
Marsil	43 6
Louāni	50 58
Tolos	43 30
Anwarp	51 28
Bruge	51 30
Craco	51 0
Prag	50 4
Dantis	55 0
Emdem	53 42
Venit	44 50
Colō	51 0

Hinged to this part of the compendium is a plate engraved on one side with the ruling planets of the 12 day hours of each day (A). The days are indicated with their symbol (i.e. the symbols for the seven planets), the hours are indicated by 12 boxes into which is inscribed the symbol of the corresponding planet. The other side is laid out as a nocturnal (B).

A) The table is labelled 'Tabula gubernacionis planetarum'. It consists of three circular scales: the two outer ones for the 12 hours of the day divided into two times six, the inner one is marked 'Dies' and shows the planetary symbols. There are two rotatable indices: a longer one for the hours, and a shorter one for the days. These seem to be later additions since they block the view through the nocturnal on the reverse. The following data can be read off:

Dies Solis (i.e. Sunday)
Sol
Mars
Mercury
Moon
Saturn
Iupiter
Venus
Sol
Mars
Mercury
Moon
Saturn
etc. for the other days of the week.

The ruling planet for the first hour of the day gives the day its name. Since there are 24 hours and seven planets the next day moves three planets further on.

B) The nocturnal consists of two circular scales and two volvelles, each with an index.

The outside scale is marked anticlockwise with the names of the months in English as follows: 'Ianiary, Februa, Marche, Aprill, Maye, Iune, Iulye, Augus, Septe, October, Nouem, Decemb'. Each month is marked with the corresponding number of days (December appears to have 31.25 days to indicate the leap year), numbered by 10 and divided to 2.

The outer volvelle has a 24-hour scale marked anticlockwise twice 1 - 12. The hours are further indicated by small teeth, 12 o'clock with an index.

The central disc is marked 'THE POVL STAR' and has an 'INDEX POLARIS'. The area around a central slot is decorated with a sun burst.

The outside of the base is engraved with a degree scale 0 - 90 - 0 - 90 - 0, starting at the east-west line, numbered by 10 and divided to 2.

In the top half of the vacant space is a double horary quadrant for unequal hours, numbered 1 - 6 - 12 and marked 'Hora planetaru<m>'.

The lower half is inscribed with a double shadow scale to the base 12, marked 'Vmbra Versa' and 'Vmbra Recta', numbered by 3 and divided to 1.

A counterchanged alidade, with the sighting vanes missing, rotates over this face. One arm is marked with a zodiacal scale.

The base of the instrument is covered with a lid which has the same decorative engraving on the inside as the plate covering the space for the compass. The engraving on the outside appears to be more refined.

The outer edge of the instrument is inscribed with the mottos 'MORA NULLA FUGACIBUS HORIS' (i.e. There is no length of stay for the fleeting hours) and 'NON QUAM DIU SED QUAM BENE' (i.e. Not as long as possible, but as good as possible).

The instrument is fitted with a suspension ring which allowed it to be suspended from a belt or perhaps to be worn on a chain around the owner's neck.

Bibliography

Michel, Henri, *Les Cadrans Solaires de Max Elscamp*, (Liège, Editions du Musée Wallonne, 1966), p. 62 with pl. XXVI.

Michel, Henri, *Catalogue des Cadrans Solaires du Musée de la Vie Wallonne*, 2 ed. (Liège, Editions du Musée Wallonne, 1974), pp. 47 f.

16 Astronomical compendium Figure 27
Horniman Museum, London

inv. no. 31.183 A
Signed and dated: Humfrey Cole 1590
Gilt brass; diameter 52 mm

This circular astronomical compendium consists of a nocturnal, a list of latitudes, a compass, and a horizontal dial for use at different latitudes.

The nocturnal consists of a circular calendrical scale and two volvelles, one of which has an index.

The outside scale is marked with the English names of the months as follows: 'Ianneuarie, Februarie, March, Aprill, Maie, Iune, Iulie, August, September, October, Nouember, December'. Each month has a scale with the corresponding number of days, numbered by 10 and divided to 2.

The outer volvelle has an hour scale marked clockwise 9 - 12 - 3. The hours are further indicated by small teeth, additionally there is a star-shaped boss at 12 o'clock., which allows the dial to be set to the appropriate date.

The inner volvelle is marked 'STELLA POLARIS OR VRSA MINOR' on a scroll and decorated with stars. It has a central slot by which the volvelle can be aligned with the pointer stars. With this construction no additional index is needed.

The inside of the lid is inscribed with a list of the latitudes of 20 cities in two circles as follows:

Exeter	50.45
Couentre	52.28
Canterburi	51.18
Notingame	53
Bath	51.26
Norwich	52.44
London	51.33
Yorcke	54
Oxford	51.47
Newcastel	55
Coulchester	52
Barwick	56
N.hampton	52.15
Edenborongh [!]	57
Cambridge	52.14
Antwerp	51.28

The signature and date 'Humfrey Cole 1590' are engraved in the centre of this list.

The base is laid out as a horizontal dial for the (marked) latitudes 50, 51, 53, 55, 57. The folding gnomon is missing. The hour lines are numbered anticlockwise IX - XII - III and divided to half-hours.

The space between the 9 o'clock and 3 o'clock line is taken up by an inset compass of which only the pin remains.

In the centre of the dial is the inscription 'This dial is ieverall for England and Scotland and for all contres ye lie east and west from them'.

The outside of the base decorated with ornamental flowers and a bird with spread wings. An inscription on the outside quotes Matthew 24,42: 'VIGILATE QVIA NESCITIS QVA HORA DOMINVS VESTER VENTVRVS SIT' (i.e. Be vigilant therefore, since you know not the hour when the Lord cometh).

The outside edge is decorated with a rope-twist design.

A suspension apparatus in the form of a ring allowed it to be suspended from a belt or perhaps to be worn on a chain around the owner's neck.

Bibliography

A Girdle Round About the Earth - Astronomical and Geographical discovery 1490-1630. Catalogue of an exhibition [held] 27 April - 30 June 1974, mounted by the Bath Festival Society and Holburne of Menstrie, (1974), p. 8, no. 31.

Figure 27   Astronomical compendium 1590 (catalogue no. 16). Reproduced by kind permission of the Horniman Museum, London.

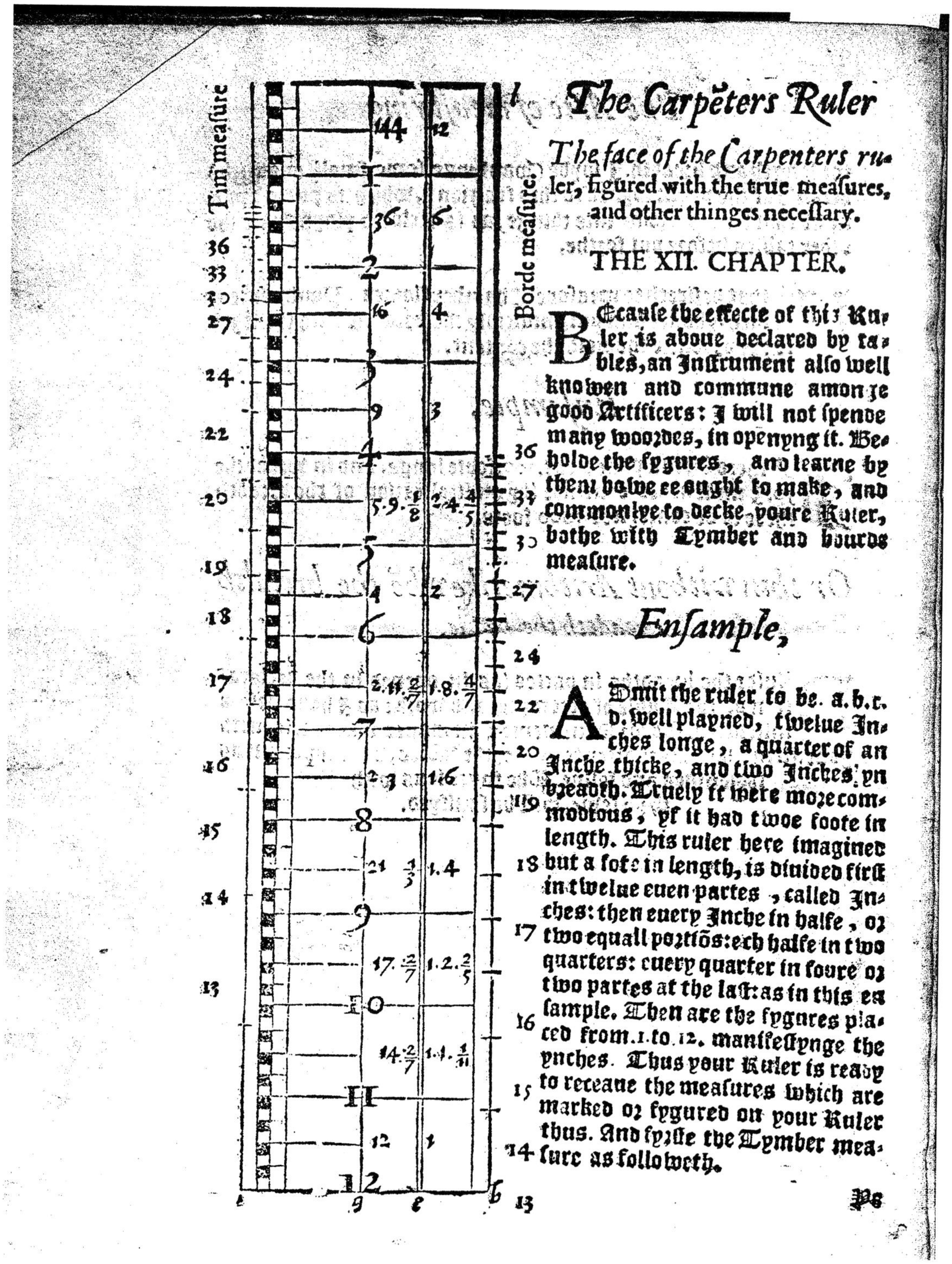

The Carpeters Ruler

The face of the Carpenters ruler, figured with the true measures, and other thinges necessary.

THE XII. CHAPTER.

Because the effecte of this Ruler is aboue declared by tables, an Instrument also well knowen and commune amonge good Artificers: I will not spende many wordes, in openyng it. Beholde the fygures, and learne by them howe ee ought to make, and commonlye to decke youre Ruler, bothe with Tymber and bourds measure.

Ensample,

Admit the ruler to be. a.b.c.d. well playned, twelue Inches longe, a quarter of an Inche thicke, and two Inches yn breadth. Truely it were more commodious, yf it had twoe foote in length. This ruler here imagined but a fote in length, is diuided first in twelue euen partes, called Inches: then euery Inche in halfe, or two equall portiōs: ech halfe in two quarters: euery quarter in foure or two partes at the last: as in this ensample. Then are the fygures placed from.1.to.12. manifestynge the ynches. Thus your Ruler is ready to receaue the measures which are marked or fygured on your Ruler thus. And fyrste the Tymber measure as followeth.

Pe

Figure 28 'The face of the carpenter's rule', Leonard Digges, Tectonicon, *published 1556, imprinted London 1570 (British Library c.127.d.15). Reproduced by kind permission of the British Library.*

Folding Rules

Four folding rules by Humphrey Cole have survived: two dated 1574 (Cambridge and London Science Museum); and two dated 1575 (Florence and Oxford).

These rules consist of two limbs hinged together so that they are foldable. They can be used with the limbs closed, fully opened, or open at different angles. The rules differ in their range of applications, but their basic design features all the requirements of a carpenter's rule as described by Leonard Digges in his *Tectonicon* of 1556 (Figure 28).

The limbs are inscribed on one side with an inch scale marked 1 - 24, thus providing a two-foot rule when fully opened. The limb with the inch scale 13 - 24 is divided to provide scales for equal parts for use with maps. The divisions differ for every instrument.

The same side of the rule is marked with scales to calculate areas and volumes of timber. For this application the limbs would also be fully open. 'BORDE MEASURE' indicates a scale which can be used to calculate the area of timber; it is typically marked 7 - 36, supplemented by a scale which provides board measures from 1 - 12 inches (marked 'B'). 'TIMBER MEASURE' indicates a scale which can be used to calculate the volume of timber, an application requiring much more mathematical knowledge. The scale is marked 9 - 36 and is supplemented by a scale providing measures from 1 - 12 inches (marked 'T'). This means that the values 7 - 12 and 9 - 12 respectively are provided twice, while no scales for measurements larger than 36 inches are given.

These supplementary scales are divided as follows:

Inches	T			B		
1	144			12		
2	36			6		
3	16			4		
4	9			3		
5	5	9	1/8	2	4	4/5
6	4			2		
7	2	11	2/7	1	8	4/7
8	2	3		1	6	
9		21	1/3	1	4	
10		17	2/7	1	2	2/5
11		14	2/7	1	1	1/11
12		12		1		

This application of the rule provides a simple method to calculate the area of timber as follows:

The width of a piece of wood is measured (for example with the two-foot rule). If it measures more than seven inches, for example 13 inches, the 'Borde measure' scale can be used directly with a pair of dividers: one foot is set into the far edge of the rule, the other is set to the mark for 13. One then simply steps with the dividers thus set along the other side of the material of which one intends to calculate the area and counts the steps. Each step equals one square foot.

If the width is smaller than 13 inches, for example seven inches, one has to use the supplementary 'B' scale and the dividers cannot be applied directly. One reads off the value given alongside the '7' on the inch scale, 2.4 4/5, i.e. 2 feet 4 inches and 4/5 of an inch. This length equals again 1 square foot. With the use of a piece of string or a chain one steps along the material and simply counts the steps.

The use of the 'Timber' and 'T' scales to determine the volume of timber is more complicated and involves the use of tables for square roots.

A degree scale 0 - 180 on the semicircular joint and an equal parts scale 500 - 0 - 500 on the inside edge of the limbs allow the rule to be used with the aide of sighting vanes as an observation instrument.

With the limbs fixed at 90° the rule can be used for measuring vertical elevations: one limb is inscribed with scales for a 'Quadrans' and a 'Quadratum Geometricum'. In use a plumb bob would have been fixed to a hole in the other limb.

Additional markings and tables are described with the individual instruments and explained in the glossary.

17 Folding Rule

Figure 29

Whipple Museum of the History of Science, Cambridge

inv. no. 3199

Signed and dated: Humfrey Côle 1574

Brass; length folded 339 mm, 65 mm wide

Side A

A two-foot rule with the limbs fully open: both limbs are inscribed with an inch scale marked 1 - 24, numbered by 1 and divided on one limb (1 - 12) to ½, 1/4 and 1/8. On the other limb (13 - 24) the scale is divided to provide scales for equal parts for use with maps; each inch is marked with the number of parts into which it is divided:

13 into 16 parts, divided to ½, 1/4, 1/8, 1/16.
14 into 32 parts, divided to ½, 1/4, 1/8, 1/16, 1/32.
15 into 64 parts, divided to ½, 1/4, 1/8, 1/16, 1/32, 1/64.
16 into 6 parts, divided to ½, 1/6.
17 into 12 parts, divided to ½, 1/6, 1/12.
18 into 24 parts, divided to ½, 1/6, 1/12, 1/24.
19 into 7 parts, divided to 1/7.
20 into 14 parts, divided to 1/7, 1/14.
21 into 28 parts, divided to 1/7, 1/14, 1/28.
22 into 10 parts, divided to ½, 1/10.
23 into 15 parts, divided to 1/3, 1/15.
24 into 20 parts, divided to 1/5, 1/10, 1/20.

The same side of the rule is marked with scales to calculate areas and volumes of timber. For this application the limbs would also be fully open. 'BORDE MEASURE' indicates a scale which can be used to calculate the area of timber, marked 7 - 36, supplemented by a scale which provides board measures from 1 - 12 inches (marked 'B'). 'TIMBER MEASURE' indicates a scale which can be used to calculate the volume of timber. It is marked 9 - 36 and is supplemented by a scale providing measures from 1 - 12 inches (marked 'T') as follows:

Inches	T			B		
1	144			12		
2	36			6		
3	16			4		
4	9			3		
5	5	9	1/8	2	4	4/5
6	4			2		
7	2	11	2/7	1	8	4/7
8	2	3		1	6	
9		21	1/3	1	4	
10		17	2/7	1	2	2/5
11		14	2/7	1	1	1/11
12		12		1		

The semicircular joint is marked with a degree scale 0 - 180. This scale is used with the limbs at variable angles where the inner edge of the movable limb serves as the index. With sighting vanes (now missing) fitted to the two circular holes on each leg (marked A, B, C, D) the rule would serve as an observation instrument.

Inside edge of both limbs

The inside edge of the limbs is inscribed with an equal part scale 500 - 0 - 500, divided to 10 and 2, the scale continuing along the joint. Fitted with sighting vanes (now missing) and with the limbs fully open the instrument would have served as a plane table alidade.

Side B

With the limbs fixed at 90° the rule can be used for measuring vertical elevations: one limb is inscribed with scales for a 'Quadrans' and a 'Quadratum Geometricum'. The quadrant scale 0 - 63 is numbered by 5 and divided to 1. The two parts of the shadow square are marked 'Latus Vmbra Versa' and 'Latus Vmbra Recta'; both are to the base 60, numbered by 5 and divided to 1. In use a plumb bob (now missing) would have been fixed to a hole in the other limb.

The instrument is signed and dated 'Humfrey Côle 1574' along the 'Quadrans' scale.

To the right of the markings for the 'Quadratum Geometricum' is a text relating to the conversion of length and area measures as follows:

'3 Barly cornes to an ynche. 12 ynches a foote. 3 foote a yarde. 5 yardes and ½ a pearche. 40 pearches in lengthe and 4 in breadthe an acre. So an acre contayneth 160 pearches. the halfe acre 80 pearches. a roode 40 pearches'.

This text is supplemented by a table giving different side lengths of an acre in perches as described by Leonard Digges (see Figure 30):

Acre	
Breadth	Length
1	160
2	80
4	40
5	32
8	20
10	16

The circular joint has a semicircle in the centre inscribed with triangles marked 'lat.3, lat.4, lat.5, lat.6, lat.10' (where 'lat.' stands for 'latus', i.e. side) and the letters a, b, d, f, g, h and i. These represent the lengths of the sides of regular polygons drawn inside a circle of the same radius as the semicircle.

Bibliography

Bennett, Jim, *A Decade of Accessions - Selected Instruments acquired by the Whipple Museum of the History of Science between 1980 and 1990*, (Cambridge, Whipple Museum, 1992), no. 1.

Johnston, Stephen, 'The Carpenter's Rule: Instruments, Practitioners and Artisans in 16th-Century England', *Proceedings of the Eleventh International Scientific Instrument Symposium*, eds Giorgio Dragoni, Anita McConnell and Gerard Turner, (Bologna 1994), pp. 39-45.

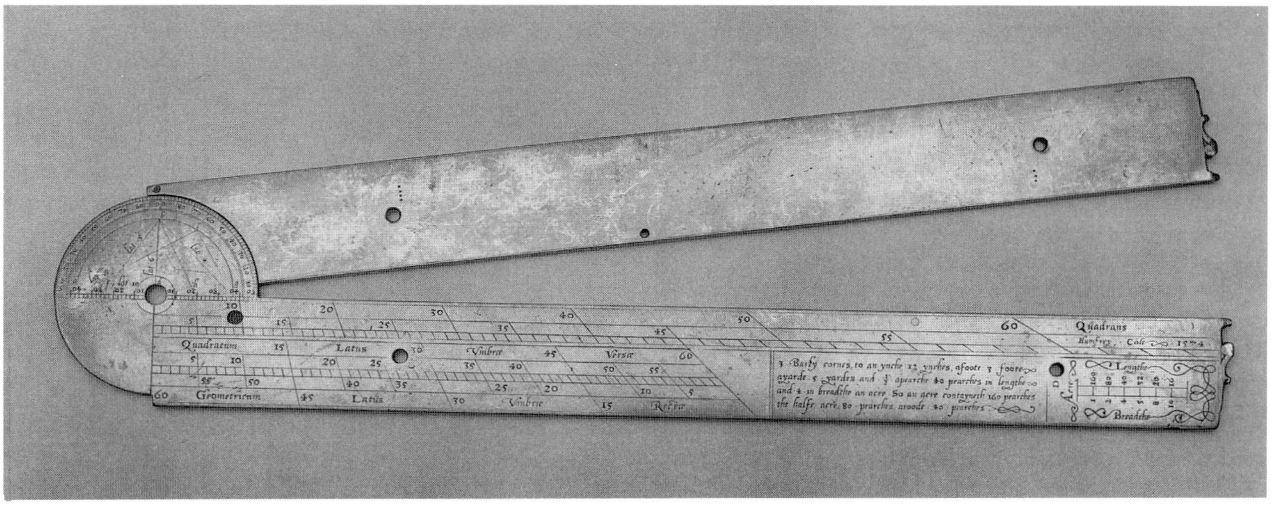

Figure 29 *Folding rule 1574 (catalogue no. 17). Reproduced by kind permission of the Whipple Museum of the History of Science, Cambridge.*

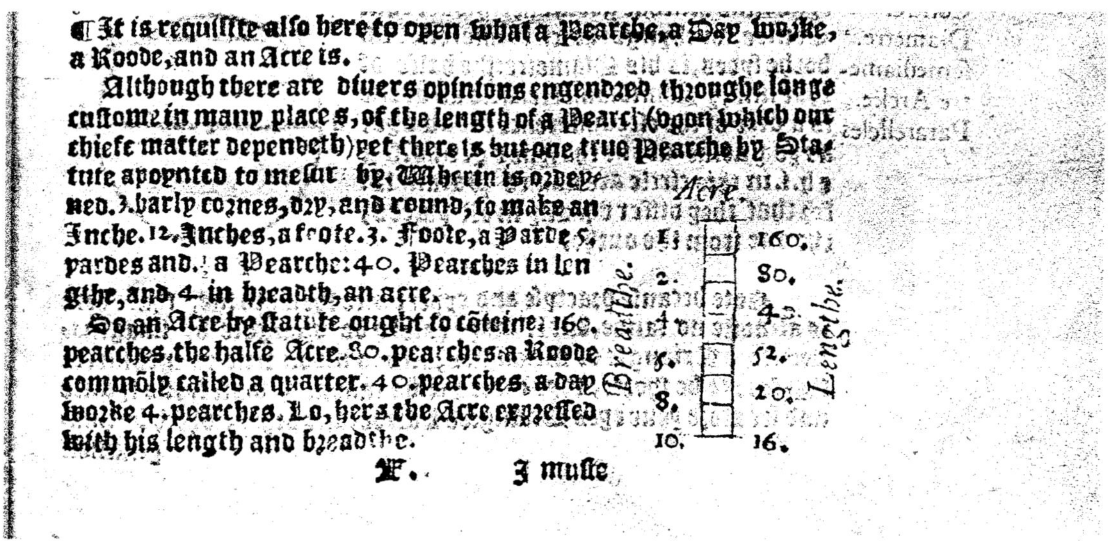

It is requisite also here to open what a Pearche, a Day worke, a Roode, and an Acre is.

Although there are diuers opinions engendred throughe longe custome in many places, of the length of a Pearch (vpon which our chiefe matter dependeth) yet there is but one true Pearche by Statute apoynted to measure by. Wherin is ordeyned. 3. barly cornes, dry, and round, to make an Inche. 12. Inches, a foote. 3. Foote, a yarde. 5. yardes and. ½ a Pearche: 40. Pearches in lengthe, and. 4. in breadth, an acre.

So an Acre by statute ought to conteine: 160. pearches. the halfe Acre. 80. pearches. a Roode commonly called a quarter. 40. pearches, a day worke 4. pearches. Lo, here the Acre expressed with his length and breadthe.

F. I muste

Figure 30 *'what a Pearche, ... a Roode, and an Acre is', Leonard Digges,* Tectonicon, *published 1556, imprinted London 1570 (British Library c.127.d.15). Reproduced by kind permission of the British Library.*

18 Folding Rule Figure 31 on Plate V
Science Museum, London
inv. no. 1984-742
Signed and dated: Humfrey Côle 1574
Brass; length folded 305 mm

This folding rule with a decorative dog's head at each end is the only instrument in the group with markings for an altitude sundial.

Side A
A two-foot rule with the limbs fully open: both limbs are inscribed with an inch scale marked 1 - 24, numbered by 1 and divided on one limb (1 - 12) to ½, 1/4 and 1/8. On the other limb (13 - 24) the scale is divided to provide scales for equal parts for use with maps as follows:
13 into 16 parts, divided to ½, 1/4, 1/8, 1/16.
14 into 32 parts, divided to ½, 1/4, 1/8, 1/16, 1/32.
15 into 64 parts, divided to ½, 1/4, 1/8, 1/16, 1/32, 1/64.
16 into 12 parts, divided to ½, 1/6, 1/12.
17 into 24 parts, divided to ½, 1/6, 1/12, 1/24.
18 into 14 parts, divided to 1/7, 1/14.
19 into 28 parts, divided to 1/7, 1/14, 1/28.
20 into 18 parts, divided to 1/3, 1/9, 1/18.
21 into 15 parts, divided to 1/3, 1/15.
22 into 10 parts, divided to 1/5, 1/10
23 into 20 parts, divided to 1/5, 1/10, 1/20.
24 into 11 parts, divided to 1/11.

The same side of the rule is marked with scales to calculate areas and volumes of timber. For this application the limbs would also be fully open. 'BORDE MEASURE' indicates a scale which can be used to calculate the area of timber; it is marked 7 - 36, supplemented by a scale which provides board measures from 1 - 12 inches (marked 'B'). 'TIMBER MEASURE' indicates a scale which can be used to calculate the volume of timber, it is marked 9 - 36 and supplemented by a scale providing measures from 1 - 12 inches (marked 'T') as follows:

Inches	T			B		
1	144			12		
2	36			6		
3	16			4		
4	9			3		
5	5	9	1/8	2	4	4/5
6	4			2		
7	2	11	2/7	1	8	4/7
8	2	3		1	6	
9		21	1/3	1	4	
10		17	2/7	1	2	2/5
11		14	2/7	1	1	1/11
12		12		1		

The semicircular joint is marked with a double degree scale 0 - 180. This scale is used with the limbs at variable angles where the inner edge of the movable limb serves as the index. With sighting vanes (now missing) fitted to the two circular holes on each leg (marked A, B, C, D) the rule would serve as an observation instrument.

Inside edge of both limbs
The inside edge of the limbs is inscribed with an equal part scale 500 - 0 - 500, divided to 10 and 2, the scale continuing along the joint. Fitted with sighting vanes (now missing) and with the limbs fully open the instrument would have served as a plane table alidade.

Side B
With the limbs fixed at 90° the rule can be used for measuring vertical elevations: one limb is inscribed with scales for a 'Quadrans' and a 'Quadratum Geometricum'. The quadrant scale 0 - 66 is numbered by 5 and divided to 1. The two parts of the shadow square are marked 'Latus Vmbra Versa' and 'Latus Vmbra Recta'; both are to the base 60, numbered by 5 and divided to 1. In use a plumb bob (now missing) would have been fixed to a hole in the other limb. The instrument is signed and dated 'Humfrey Côle 1574' to the right-hand side of the shadow square.
To the right of the markings for the 'Quadratum Geometricum' is a text relating to the conversion of length and area measures as follows:
'3 Barly cornes to an ynche. 12 ynches a foote. 3 foote a yarde. 5 yardes and ½ a pearche. 40 pearches in lengthe and 4 in breadthe an acre. So an acre contayneth 160 pearches. the halfe acre 80 pearches. a roode 40 pearches'.
This text is supplemented by a table giving different side lengths of an acre in perches:

Acre	
Breadth	Length
1	160
2	80
4	40
5	32
8	20
10	16

This instrument has additional markings as an altitude sundial for latitude *c.* 52° with the limbs fixed at a 90° angle. The limb, which does not have the quadrant with the shadow square, is marked together with the joint with lines for equal hours, numbered 7/5, 8/4, 9/3, 10/2, 11/1, 12 with divisions for 15 minutes. A zodiacal scale along the 12 o'clock line is engraved with the symbols of the signs, each sign divided to 10°. The dial is marked 'The houres of the daye and what Signe the sonne is in at all tymes'.
A table to the left gives the dates of the sun's entry into a particular zodiacal sign. The following dates can be read off:

Aquarius	11 January
Pisces	10 February
Aries	11 March
Taurus	11 April
Gemini	12 May
Cancer	12 June

Leo	14 July
Virgo	14 August
Libra	14 September
Scorpio	14 October
Sagittarius	13 November
Capricornus	12 December

Two different ways of using this part of the instrument as an altitude dial have been established so far.

a) The rule would have been placed in a position where the limb with the dial markings would have been vertical, the other limb horizontal. A pin gnomon (now missing) would have been fixed to a hole in the horizontal limb and the instrument would have been directed towards the sun. The time could then have been read off at the point where the shadow intersects the appropriate date, indicated by the position of the sun in the zodiac.

b) The limb with the hour markings would have been fitted with two sighting vanes (now missing) and a plumb bob would have been fitted to a hole in the same limb. The instrument would then have been used like a quadrant, so that the altitude of the sun would have been measured by means of the sighting vanes; the time could then have been read off at the point where the plumb bob would have intersected with the appropriate line for the sun's position in the zodiac (see Figure 32).

Bibliography

Johnston, Stephen, 'The Carpenter's Rule: Instruments, Practitioners and Artisans in 16th-Century England', *Proceedings of the Eleventh International Scientific Instrument Symposium*, eds Giorgio Dragoni, Anita McConnell and Gerard Turner, (Bologna 1994), pp. 39-45.

Sotheby's, London Sale Catalogue, 12 June 1984, lot 329.

Vaughan, Denys, A Very Artificial Workman: The Altitude Sundials of Humphrey Cole, in: *Making Instruments Count. Essays on Historical Scientific Instruments presented to Gerard L'Estrange Turner*, eds R.G.W. Anderson, J.A. Bennett, W.F. Ryan, Aldershot (Variorum), 1993, pp. 191-200, esp. pp. 199f.

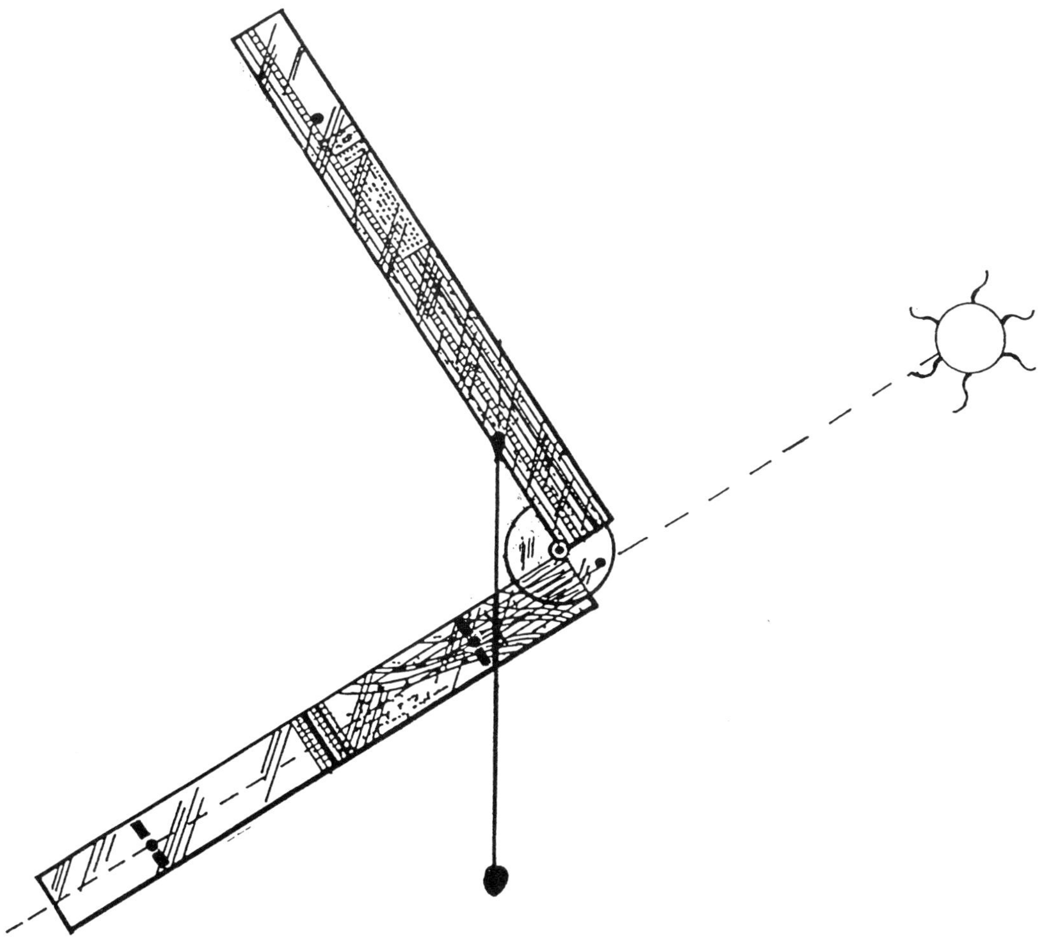

Figure 32 The use of the sundial on the 1574 folding rule with a plumb bob. Drawing reproduced by kind permission of Denys Vaughan from his article 'A Very Artificial Workman: The Altitude Sundials of Humphrey Cole', Making Instruments Count. Essays on Historical Scientific Instruments presented to Gerard L'Estrange Turner, *edited R.G.W. Anderson, J.A. Bennett, W.F. Ryan, (Aldershot, Variorum, 1993), pp. 191-200.*

19 Folding Rule Figure 33

Museum of the History of Science, Oxford
inv. no. 49,631 (previously 50-41)
Signed and dated: Humfrey Côle 1575
Brass; length folded 305 mm

Side A
A two-foot rule with the limbs fully open: both limbs are inscribed with an inch scale marked 1 - 24, numbered by 1 and divided on one limb (1 - 12) to ½, 1/4 and 1/8. On the other limb (13 - 24) the scale is divided to provide scales for equal parts for use with maps as follows:
13 into 16 parts, divided to ½, 1/4, 1/8, 1/16.
14 into 32 parts, divided to ½, 1/4, 1/8, 1/16, 1/32.
15 into 64 parts, divided to ½, 1/4, 1/8, 1/16, 1/32, 1/64.
16 into 36 parts, divided to 1/6, 1/12, 1/36.
17 into 24 parts, divided to ½, 1/6, 1/12, 1/24.
18 into 42 parts, divided to 1/7, 1/14, 1/42.
19 into 28 parts, divided to 1/7, 1/14, 1/28.
20 into 18 parts, divided to 1/3, 1/9, 1/18.
21 into 15 parts, divided to 1/3, 1/15.
22 into 20 parts, divided to 1/5, 1/10, 1/20.
23 into 22 parts, divided to ½, 1/22.
24 into 26 parts, divided to ½, 1/26.

The same side of the rule is marked with scales to calculate areas and volumes of timber. For this application the limbs would also be fully open. 'BORDE MEASURE' indicates a scale which can be used to calculate the area of timber; it is marked 7 - 36, supplemented by a scale which provides board measures from 1 - 12 inches (marked 'B'). 'TIMBER MEASURE' indicates a scale which can be used to calculate the volume of timber, it is marked 9 - 36 and supplemented by a scale providing measures from 1 - 12 inches (marked 'T') as follows:

Inches	T			B		
1	144			12		
2	36			6		
3	16			4		
4	9			3		
5	5	9	1/8	2	4	4/5
6	4			2		
7	2	11	2/7	1	8	4/7
8	2	3		1	6	
9		21	1/3	1	4	
10		17	2/7	1	2	2/5
11		14	2/7	1	1	1/11
12		12		1		

The semicircular joint is marked with a double degree scale 0 - 180. This scale is used with the limbs at variable angles where the inner edge of the movable limb serves as the index. With sighting vanes (now missing) fitted to the two circular holes on each leg (marked A, B, C, D) the rule would serve as an observation instrument.

Inside edge of both limbs
The inside edge of the limbs is inscribed with an equal part scale 500 - 0 - 500, divided to 10 and 2, the scale continuing along the joint. Fitted with sighting vanes (now missing) and with the limbs fully open the instrument would have served as a plane table alidade.

Side B
With the limbs fixed at 90° the rule can be used for measuring vertical elevations: one limb is inscribed with scales for a 'Quadrans' and a 'Quadratum Geometricum'. The quadrant scale 0 - 66 is numbered by 5 and divided to 1. The two parts of the shadow square are marked 'Latus Vmbra Versa' and 'Latus Vmbra Recta'; both are to the base 60, numbered by 5 and divided to 1. In use a plumb bob (now missing) would have been fixed in a hole in the other limb.
To the right-hand side of the shadow square the instrument is signed and dated 'Humfrey Côle 1575'.

Bibliography

Johnston, Stephen, 'The Carpenter's Rule: Instruments, Practitioners and Artisans in 16th-Century England', in: *Proceedings of the Eleventh International Scientific Instrument Symposium*, eds Giorgio Dragoni, Anita McConnell and Gerard Turner (Bologna 1994), pp. 39-45

Turner, Gerard L'E., 'Mathematical Instrument-Making in London in the Sixteenth Century', *English Map-Making 1500-1650*, ed. Sarah Tyacke (London 1983), pp. 93-106, esp. p.103 with pl. 51.

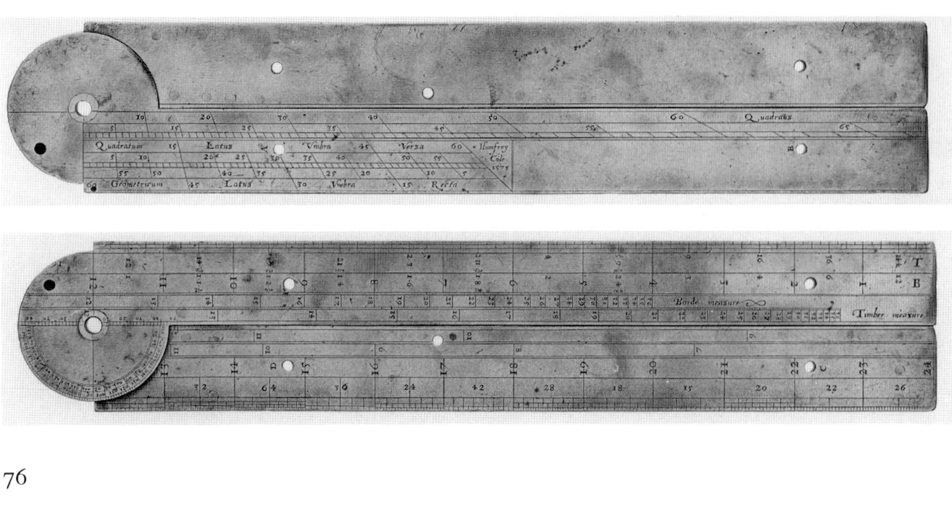

Figure 33 Folding rule 1575 (catalogue no. 19). Reproduced with kind permission of the Museum of the History of Science, Oxford (photo Giles Hudson)

20 Folding Rule Figure 34
Museo di Storia della Scienza, Florence
inv. no. 2527
Signed and dated: Humfrey Côle 1575
Brass; length folded 305 mm

Side A
A two-foot rule with the limbs fully open: both limbs are inscribed with an inch scale marked 1 - 24, numbered by 1 and divided on one limb (1 - 12) to ½, 1/4 and 1/8. On the other limb (13 - 24) the scale is divided to provide scales for equal parts for use with maps as follows:
13 into 16 parts, divided to ½, 1/4, 1/8, 1/16.
14 into 32 parts, divided to ½, 1/4, 1/8, 1/16, 1/32.
15 into 64 parts, divided to ½, 1/4, 1/8, 1/16, 1/32, 1/64.
16 into 12 parts, divided to ½, 1/4, 1/12.
17 into 24 parts, divided to ½, 1/6, 1/12, 1/24.
18 into 18 parts, divided to 1/3, 1/9, 1/18.
19 into 20 parts, divided to 1/5, 1/10, 1/20.
20 into 30 parts, divided to 1/5, 1/15, 1/30.
21 into 14 parts, divided to 1/7, 1/14.
22 into 28 parts, divided to 1/7, 1/14, 1/28.
23 into 21 parts, divided to 1/3, 1/21.
24 into 11 parts, divided into 1/11.

The same side of the rule is marked with scales to calculate areas and volumes of timber. For this application the limbs would also be fully open. 'BORDE MEASURE' indicates a scale which can be used to calculate the area of timber; it is marked 7 - 36, supplemented by a scale which provides board measures from 1 - 12 inches (marked 'B'). 'TIMBER MEASURE' indicates a scale which can be used to calculate the volume of timber, it is marked 9 - 36 and supplemented by a scale providing measures from 1 - 12 inches (marked 'T') as follows:

Inches	T			B		
1	144			12		
2	36			6		
3	16			4		
4	9			3		
5	5	9	1/8	2	4	4/5
6	4			2		
7	2	11	2/7	1	8	4/7
8	2	3		1	6	
9		21	1/3	1	4	
10		17	2/7	1	2	2/5
11		14	2/7	1	1	1/11
12		12		1		

The semicircular joint is marked with a double degree scale 0 - 180. This scale is used with the limbs at variable angles where the inner edge of the movable limb serves as the index. Different from the other surviving rules this instrument still has four foldable sights which it serves as an observation instrument.

Inside edge of both limbs
The inside edge of the limbs is inscribed with an equal part scale 500 - 0 - 500, divided to 10 and 2, the scale continuing along the joint. Using the folding sighting vanes and with the limbs fully open the instrument serves as a plane table alidade.

Side B
With the limbs fixed at 90° the rule can be used for measuring vertical elevations: one limb is inscribed with scales for a 'Quadrans' and a 'Quadratum Geometricum'. The quadrant scale 0 - 65 is numbered by 5 and divided to 1. The two parts of the shadow square are marked 'Latus Vmbra Versa' and 'Latus Vmbra Recta'; both are to the base 60, numbered by 5 and divided to 1. In use a plumb bob (now missing) would have been fixed in a hole in the other limb.
To the right-hand side of the shadow square the instrument is signed and dated 'Humfrey Côle 1575'.

Bibliography

Johnston, Stephen, 'The Carpenter's Rule: Instruments, Practitioners and Artisans in 16th-Century England', *Proceedings of the Eleventh International Scientific Instrument Symposium*, eds Giorgio Dragoni, Anita McConnell and Gerard Turner, (Bologna 1994), pp. 39-45.
Righini Bonelli, Maria Luisa, *Il Museo di Storia della Scienza a Firenze*, (Milan 1968), p. 165, no. 123 and p. 181, no. 291. (The same instrument is described under two different numbers).
Turner, Gerard L'E., 'Misurazione del Tempo', *Gli Strumenti*, (Milan 1990), p. 202.

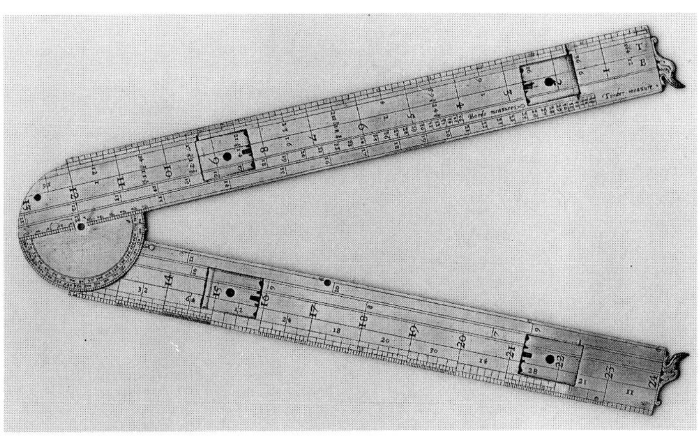

Figure 34 Folding rule 1575 (catalogue no. 20). Reproduced by kind permission of the Istituto e Museo di Storia della Scienza di Firenze (photo Franca Principe).

Folding Gunners' Rules

The three surviving gunners' rules by Humphrey Cole offer a wide range of applications beyond those described in the section 'Folding rules' which make them a valuable instrument in gunnery and trade.

The 'E Canon' or 'Eliza' which Cole mentions in his list of cannons has not been found in any other context, except in Samuel Cleaveland's notes on 'Great ordnances' for 1574. Cleaveland, an artillery officer with an interest in the history of artillery, died in 1794.

21 Folding Gunner's Rule Figure 35 on Plate V
British Museum, London
inv. no. MLA 1912,11-1.1
Signed and dated: H Côle 1575
Brass; length folded 188 mm, 32 mm wide

This rule can only be used at variable angles up to 90°, since a folding skeleton square fixed to the inside of the limbs prevents it from being unfolded further.

It consists of two foldable limbs hollowed on the inside to accommodate a folding square and four tablets (two in each limb) engraved on all sides. One limb has folding sights on the outside edge.

The use of the instrument is best summarised in Cole's own words inscribed on the outside edge of one of the limbs: 'This Instrument is a rule a square a peare of Compasses A quadrant to knowe y[e] howres heights and difrances of any thinge y[e] shotinge of Ordenance to measure'.

Side A
Both edges are divided to provide scales for equal parts for use with maps as follows:
7 parts, divided to 1/7.
54 parts, divided to ½, 1/6, 1/18, 1/54.
44 parts, divided to ½, 1/22, 1/44.
42 parts, divided to 1/3, 1/21, 1/42.
30 parts, divided to 1/3, 1/15, 1/30.
13 parts, divided to 1/13.
64 parts, divided to ½, 1/4, 1/8, 1/16, 1/32, 1/64.
24 parts, divided to ½, 1/6, 1/12, 1/24.
40 parts, divided to ½, 1/10, 1/20, 1/40.
36 parts, divided to 1/3, 1/9, 1/18, 1/36.
28 parts, divided to ½, 1/4, 1/28.
27 parts, divided to 1/3, 1/9, 1/27.
51 parts, divided to 1/17, 1/51.
38 parts, divided to 1/19, 1/38.
46 parts, divided to 1/23, 1/46.
58 parts, divided to 1/29, 1/58.
62 parts, divided to 1/31, 1/62.
33 parts, divided to 1/11, 1/33.
34 parts, divided to 1/17, 1/34.
35 parts, divided to 1/7, 1/35.
39 parts, divided to 1/13, 1/39.
26 parts, 1/13, 1/26.
45 parts, 1/15. 1/45.
50 parts, divided to 1/10, 1/50.
The field for 34 is also inscribed with a 'B'.
The apex is inscribed 'Timber and ynches of platt measure withe manye other vses'.
A quarter of the circular joint is inscribed with a 90° scale, numbered by 10 and divided to 2. This scale is used with the movable arm as an index to indicate the angle of separation of the limbs.
Near the ends of the limbs the positions of four stars are given; the inscriptions are now rather worn. The values in the first column seem to indicate the position of the sun when it has the same declination as the listed star, the second column gives the right ascensions of the listed stars (in brackets the modern identifications):

Pleyad<us>	7	[Cancer]	50	(η Tauri)
{Al}gomey{sa}	15	[Aries]	109	(α Canis Minoris)
Arctur<us>	11	[Gemini]	20{o?}	(α Boötes)
Aquila	19	[Aries]	29{o?}	(α Aquilae)

The signature and date 'H Côle 1575' are engraved on the outside edge of the right arm with the two folding sights. Next to them is the inscription: 'The haightes and waightes of Ordenance'. This refers to scales on side B.

Side B
The sections of the right and left limbs closer to the joint are inscribed with tables used in gunnery.
On the left limb is a table with entries for the type of cannon, its weight and the diameter of the barrel.

The Names of Ordenance	[Howe] Moche euery Pece wayethe	Hie y[e] pece in the mouthe
Robin<e>t	200	1 ¼
Fawco<ne>t	500	2
Fawco<n>	800	2 ½
Mynio<n>	1100	3 ¼
Sacar	1500	3 ½
D<emi>cull	3000	4 ¼
Cull{uerine}	4000	5 ½
D<emi> Can<on>	6000	6 ½
Canon	7000	8
E Can{on}	8000	7
Basilis{co}	9000	8 ¾

This is continued on the right limb with a table for the diameter of the bullet in inches, the powder needed for every shot in pounds, the distance where the bullet first hits the ground when fired from a horizontal barrel, in scores by paces (here mathematical paces i.e. one pace equals 5 feet), and the weight of every bullet in pounds. This table is very similar, but not identical to one found on the Woolwich rule (catalogue no. 23).

Maney Inches hye the bullet is	Howe Maney lb of powder euery pece shot<s>	Maney Scores at pointe blancke	Maney pounde euery Shote wayeth
1	½		1
1 ¾	2	14	2
2 ¼	2 ½	16	2 ½
3	4 ½	17	4 ½
3 ¼	5	18	5
4	9	20	9
5 ¼	18	25	18
6 ¼	28	28	30
7 ¾	44	20	60
6 ¾	20	20	42
8 ½	60	21	60

Further out from the table on the right limb is a text also to be found on the folding rules in Cambridge, London (Science Museum) and Woolwich (catalogue nos. 17, 18 and 23) concerning the conversion of length and area measures as follows:
'3 Barly cornes to an ynche. 12 ynches a foote. 3 foote a yarde. 5 yardes and ½ a pearche. 40 pearches in lengthe and 4 in breadthe an acre. So an acre conteynethe 160 pearches. the halfe acre 80 pearches. a roode 40 pearches'. This text is supplemented by a table giving different side lengths of an acre in perches. This table is also to be found on the three afore-mentioned rules.

Acre	
Breadth	Length
1	160
2	80
4	40
5	32
8	20
10	16

Further out on the left arm is a scale for timber measurement in feet, inches and fractions of inches. It is marked 'Square ynches of the timber'. The 'partes' scale is rather worn.

		Foote Inches	partes
1	144		
2	36		
3	16		
4	9		
5	5	9	3/25
6	4		
7	2	11	2/7
8	2	3	
9	0	21	1/3
	10	17	2/7
	11	14	2/7
	12	13	
	13	10	1/5
	14	8	13/10
	15	7	2/3
	16	6	3/4
	17	6	
	18	5	1/3
	19	4	25/32
	20	4	5/16
	21	3	11/12
	22	3	4/7
	23	3	1/4
	24	3	
	25	2	3/4
	26	2	9/16
	27	2	3/8
	28	2	1/5
	29	2	1/16
	30	1	11/12
	31	1	4/5
	32	1	11/16
	33	1	12/20
	34	1	½
	35	1	13/32
	36	1	1/3

The circular joint is inscribed with the dates of the entry of the sun into a particular sign. The sun is represented by its effigy, the signs by their symbols. The English names of the months are given in abbreviation. It is marked 'The entrauue of ye so<n>ne in the 12 signes'. The column for the months is labelled 'MONTT', the days as 'DAII', the sun as 'SON' and the signes as 'SIG'.
The following dates can be read off:

11 January	Aquarius
10 February	Pisces
11 March	Aries
11 April	Taurus
12 Mai	Gemini
12 June	Cancer
14 July	Leo
14 August	Virgo
14 September	Libra
14 October	Scorpio
13 November	Sagittarius
12 December	Capricorn

When the limbs are completely opened a folding quadrate is fully spread. On the upper side it is inscribed with a double degree scale 0 - 90 , 0 - 90, numbered by 10 and divided to 5, 1 and 1/5.
The underside has a shadow scale inscribed 'Latus Vmbrae Rectae' and Latus Vmbrae Versae' with two different scales: one 0 - 12, numbered by 3, and the other 0 - 60, numbered by 5 and divided to 1 and 1/3.
Four leaves inscribed on both sides can be folded out from the hollowed part of the limbs when the limbs are fully spread. The all have one small hole at the far end to facilitate opening them out.

They are described as follows:
1-2) left-hand upper leaf side a and b;
3-4) left-hand lower leaf side a and b;
5-6) right-hand lower leaf side a and b;
7-8) right-hand upper leaf side a and b.

Leaves 1 - 6 have a table for the solar altitude for every 30° for the hours 'ANTE MER' and 'POST MERI', i.e. for every hour of the day. The zodiacal signs are represented by their symbols and are given in the following table in abbreviations. There are also small strokes after the values which may stand for fractions, but have not been deciphered. Cole obviously confused the table for Aries and Libra with the one for Cancer and Gemini and just repeated the values given there, so that the values for Aries and Libra are missing.

AM			11	10	9	8	7	6	5	4
PM		12	1	2	3	4	5	6	7	8
30	Cnc	62	59	53	45	36	27	18	9	1
20	10	61	59	53	45	36	27	17	9	1
10	20	60	58	52	44	35	26	17	8	0
Gem	Leo	58	56	50	43	34	24	15	6	0
20	10	56	54	48	41	32	23	13	4	0
10	20	53	51	46	38	36	20	11	2	0
Tau	Vir	50	48	43	35	27	18	8	0	
20	10	46	44	39	32	24	15	6	0	
10	20	42	40	36	29	21	12	3	0	
Ari	Lib	62	59	53	45	36	27	18	9	1
20	10	61	59	53	45	36	27	17	9	1
10	20	60	58	52	44	35	26	17	8	0
Psc	Sco	27	25	21	15	8	0			
20	10	23	22	18	13	5	0			
10	20	20	19	15	10	3	0			
Aqu	Sgt	18	17	13	8	1				
20	10	16	14	11	6	0				
10	20	15	14	10	5	0				
Cpr	30	15	13	10	5	0				

The right-hand side of leaf 5 is engraved with the right ascension of five named stars as follows (in brackets the modern identifications):

Scheder	4 ½	(α Cassiopeiae)
Ras Algol	41	(α Persei)
Alhayot	71½	(α Aurigae)
Wega	274	(α Lyrae)
Benanaz	203	(η Ursae Maioris)

Leaves seven and eight are marked with a table for the entry of the sun into a particular zodiacal sign and the right ascension of the beginning of each zodiacal sign measured from the first point of Aries along the equator.
The signs are represented by their symbols. The dates given are all one day earlier than in the table described above except for June, which is identical, and the dates for January and February which are two days earlier. The following values can be read off:

10 March	Aries	0	
10 April	Taurus	28	
11 May	Gemini	57	
12 June	Cancer	90	
13 July	Leo	122	
13 August	Virgo	152	
13 September	Libra	180	
13 October	Scorpio	207	
12 November	Sagittarius	37	(recte: 237)
11 December	Capricorn	270	
9 January	Aquarius	302	
8 February	Pisces	332	

Bibliography

Gunther, R.T., 'The Great Astrolabe and other Scientific Instruments of Humphrey Cole', *Archaeologia* 76 (1927), pp. 296-298.

Ward, F.A.B., *A Catalogue of European Scientific Instruments in the Department of Medieval and Later Antiquities of the British Museum* (London 1981), p. 105, no. 310.

22 Folding Gunner's Rule Figure 36
British Museum, London
inv no. MLA 1912,11-1.1
Signed: Humfray Coolle Mad This
Undated
Brass; length 320mm, width 28 mm

When closed this instrument resembles a large pair of compasses, with flat limbs inscribed on all sides and a highly decorated hollowed joint.
One limb has foldable sights on the outside edge, one of which is missing.
When fully opened to 90°, further plates, two skeletonised folding geometrical squares and a third arm with a fiducial edge and a folding sight with a spike can be folded out from inside the hollow limbs. Even in the upright position, this sight slides into the slot in the upper side of one limb. A second sight arranged in the same way is broken off.
A movable ring around the joint with a small hole suggests that a plumb bob was fitted to the instrument.
In contrast to the scales found on other Humphrey Cole instruments, those found here are inaccurately engraved and laid out.

Side A
On one limb a 9¾ inch scale, numbered by 1. Each section is divided to 32 parts and consecutively numbered by 4 up to 312.
On the edge of this limb and on the face and edge of the other limb are the scales usually found on folding rules for calculating areas and volumes:
A scale for board measure, marked 'Borde measure', and a scale for timber measure, marked 'Tim measure'. The board scale runs from 13 to 36, the timber scale from 13 to 36. Both scales are supplemented by scales providing the board

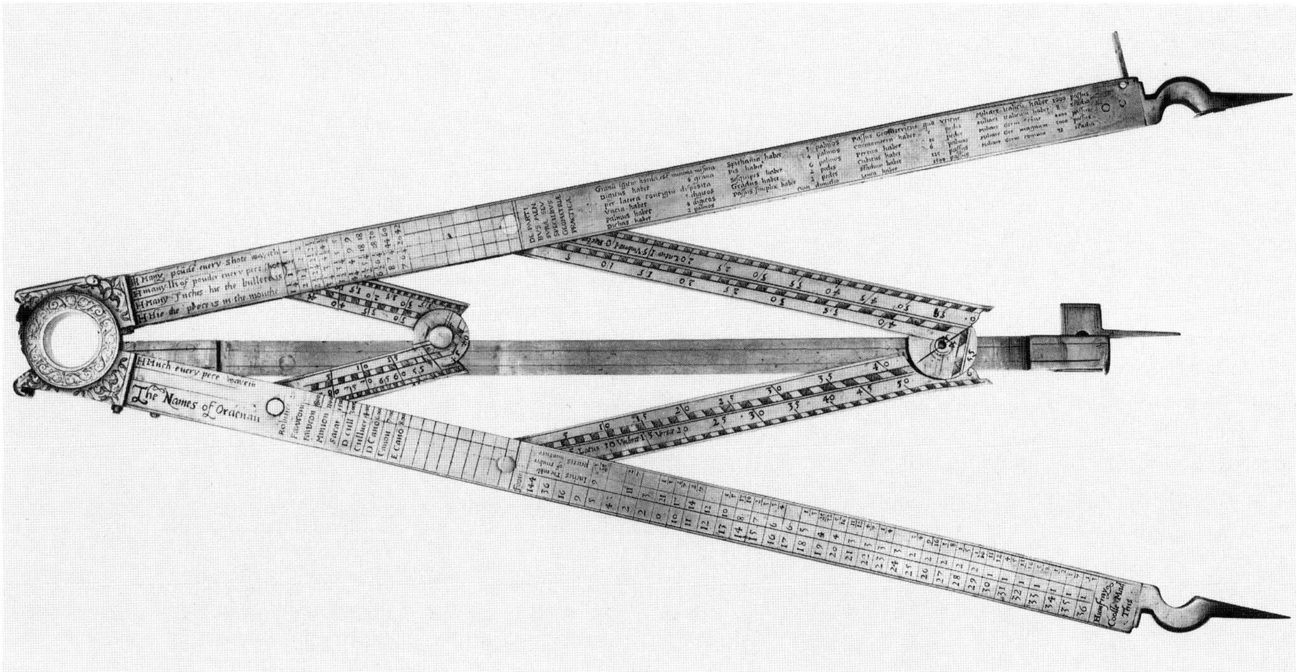

Figure 36 Folding gunner's rule (catalogue no. 22). Reproduced by kind permission of the Trustees of the British Museum.

and timber measures from 1 to 11 inches, but in this case only represented by plain boxes. They are given on one limb as follows:

144			12	
36			6	
16			4	
9			3	
5	9	1/8	2.4	4/5
4			2	
2	11	2/7	1.8	4/7
2	3		1.6	
	21	1/3	1.4	
	17	2/7	1.2	2/5
	14	2/7	1.1	1/11

Side B

Over both limbs a list of cannons 'The Names of Ordenan' (a); the weight of every cannon 'H Much euery pece wayeth' (b); the diameter of the barrel 'H Hie die piece is in the mouthe' (c); the diameter height of each bullet in inches 'H Many Inches hie the bullett is' (d); the amount of powder needed for each shot in pound 'H many lb of powder euery pece shot' (e); and how many pounds each bullet weighs 'H Many pou<n>de euery shote wayeth' (f).

a	b	c	d	e	f
Robinet	200	1 ¼	1	½	1
Fawconet	500	2	1 ¾	2	2
Fawcon	800	2 ½	2 ¼	2 ½	2 ½
Minion	1100	3 ¼	3	4 ½	4 ½
Sacar	1500	3 ½	3 ¼	5	5
D cull	3000	4 ¼	4	9	9
Culluer	4000	5 ½	5 ¼	18	18
D Cano	6000	6 ½	6 ¼	28	30
Canon	7000	8	7 ¾	44	60
E Canon	8000	7	6 ¾	20	42

The 'Basilisco', normally to be found in Cole's list, is not named, although there is space for more entries in the list. Below this list on the face and edge of the left limb is 'The table of timber measure' in feet, inches and fractions of inches as follows:

	Foote	Inches	Partes
1	144		
2	36		
3	16		
4	9		
5	5	9	3/25
6	4		
7	2	11	2/7
8	2	3	
9	0	21	1/3
	10	17	2/7
	11	14	2/7
	12	12	
	14	8	13/10
	15	7	2/3
	16	6	3/4
	17	6	
	18	5	1/3
	19	4	25/32
	20	4	5/16
	21	3	11/12
	22	3	4/7
	23	3	1/4
	24	3	

25	2	3/4
26	2	9/16
26	2	9/16
27	2	3/8
28	2	1/5
29	2	1/16
30	1	11/12
31	1	4/5
32	1	11/16
33	1	5/8
34	1	½
35	1	3/7
36	1	1/3

Inscribed on the left-hand column beneath the figures is the inscription 'SQVARE YNCHES OF THE TYMBRE'.

The signature and the date 'Humfray Coolle Mad This' are below this list close to the pointed ends of the limb.

On the face of the other limb are scales for the conversion of measures in Latin, titled 'DE PARTIBVS MENSVRAE SEV SPECIEBVS GEOMETRIAE PRACTICAE, as follows:

Granu<m> igitur hordei, est minima me<n>sura

Digitus habet	4 grana
per latera contigue disposita	
Vncia habet	3 digitos
Palmus habet	4 digitos
Dichas habet	2 palmos
Spithama habet	3 palmos
Pes habet	4 palmos
Sequipes habet	6 palmos
Gradus habet	2 pedes
Passus simplex	2 pedes cum dimidio
Passus Geometricus quo Vtitur	
Cosmometra habet	5 pedes
Pertica habet	10 pedes
Cubitus habet	6 palmos
Stadium habet	125 passus
Leuca habet	1500 passus
Miliare Italicum habet	1000 passus
Miliare Italicum habet	8 stadia
Miliare Germ cont	4000 passus
Miliare Ger magnum	5000 passus
Miliare Germ com<m>une	32 stadia

When the limbs are completely opened, two folding quadrates are fully spread.

The larger one is marked with a shadow scale inscribed 'Latus Vmbrae Rectae' and 'Latus Vmbrae Versae' with two different scales: one 0 - 60 - 0, the other 0 - 45 - 0. Both scales are numbered by 5 and divided to 1. The same scales are inscribed on the other side, but not labelled. The smaller quadrate has a scale 0 - 90 and 0 - 45 on one side and a scale 0 - 90 on the other side.

Bibliography

Gunther, R.T., 'The Great Astrolabe and other Scientific Instruments of Humphrey Cole', *Archaeologia* 76 (1927), pp. 294-296.

Ward, F.A.B., *A Catalogue of European Scientific Instruments in the Department of Medieval and Later Antiquities of the British Museum* (London 1981), p. 105, no. 311.

23 Folding Rule — Figures 37 and 38 on Plate VI

Museum of Artillery, Woolwich

inv. no. XXIV.200

Signed: H C

Undated

Brass; length folded 166 mm, 32 mm wide

This very elaborate folding rule, which has so far been described as unsigned, can be used for a variety of applications. It consists of a one-foot rule, scales for calculating areas and volume of timber, the angles of regular polygons, a geometrical quadrant, and several tables for applications in gunnery and measurement conversions.

Side A

With the limbs fully open the instrument is marked as a one-foot rule with an inch scale 1 - 12, numbered by 1 and divided to 1/2, 1/4 and 1/8. On the other edge this scale is further divided to provide scales for equal parts for use with maps; each inch is marked with the number of parts into which it is divided as follows:

1 into 16 parts, divided to 1/2, 1/4, 1/8, 1/16.
2 into 32 parts, divided to 1/2, 1/4, 1/8, 1/16, 1/32.
3 into 64 parts, divided to 1/2, 1/4, 1/8, 1/16, 1/32, 1/64.
4 into 12 parts, divided to 1/2, 1/6, 1/12.
5 into 24 parts, divided to 1/2, 1/6, 1/12, 1/24.
6 into 10 parts, divided to 1/2, 1/10.
7 into 15 parts, divided to 1/3, 1/15.
8 into 20 parts, divided to 1/5, 1/10, 1/20.
9 into 14 parts, divided to 1/7, 1/14.
10 into 28 parts, divided to 1/7, 1/14, 1/28.
11 into 9 parts, divided to 1/3, 1/9.
12 into 11 parts, divided to 1/11.

Side A and the outside edge

Inscribed with a scale for board measure, marked 'BORDE MEASURE', and a scale for timber measure, marked '{TIMBER} MEASURE'. The 'TIMBER' was obviously inscribed on the outside of a now missing sighting vane. Both scales run from 13 to 36 and are supplemented by scales providing the board and timber measures from 1 to 12 inches (marked 'B' and 'T' respectively), given within this scale as follows:

Inches	T			B		
1	144			12		
2	36			6		
3	16			4		
4	9			3		
5	5	9	1/8	2	4	4/5

6	4			2		
7	2	11	2/7	1	8	4/7
8	2		3	1	6	
9		21	1/3	1	4	
10		17	2/7	1	2	2/5
11		14	2/7	1	1	1/11
12		12		1		

The angles of regular polygons are indicated on the semicircular joint as 3, 4, 6, 8, and 12. This scale is used with the movable arm serving as an index. The following angles can be determined:

triangle: 60°
square: 90°
hexagon: 120°
octagon: 135°
duodecon: 150°

Side B

The circular joint is inscribed with, and marked as, a 'Geometrical Quadrant'.

The shadow square to the base 12 is numbered by 3, divided to 1, and is marked 'CONTRARY S[HADOW]' and 'RYGHT SHADO[W]'. An inscribed quadrant scale marked with a degree scale 0 - 90 is numbered by 10 and divided to 2 by alternate shading. Through the corner of the shadow scale and the 45° of the quadrant scale runs a line marked 'Line of leavel'.

A multiplication scale for 9, 17, 18, 19 and 20 is inscribed over both closed limbs as follows:

9	17	18	19	20	1
18	34	36	38	40	2
27	51	54	57	60	3
36	68	72	76	80	4
45	85	90	95	100	5
54	102	108	114	120	6
63	119	126	133	140	7
72	136	144	152	160	8
81	153	162	171	180	9
90	170	180	190	200	10
99	187	198	209	220	11
108	204	216	228	240	12
117	221	234	247	260	13
126	238	252	266	280	14
135	255	270	285	300	15
144	272	288	304	320	16
153	289	306	323	340	17
162	306	324	342	360	18
171	323	342	361	380	19
180	340	360	380	400	20
270	510	540	570	600	30
360	680	720	760	800	40
450	850	900	950	1000	50
540	1020	1080	1090	1200	60
630	1190	1260	1330	1400	70
720	1360	1440	1520	1600	80
810	1530	1620	1710	1800	90
900	1700	1800	1900	2000	100

Further out a table for wool weights in cloves, stones and sacks (marked 'Woll Waightes') is inscribed over both closed limbs as follows:

7^{lb} is a claue	14^{lb} is a stone
26 claue is	½ a sacke
13 stone is	½ a sacke
52 claue is	a sacke
26 stone is	a sacke
364^{lb} is	a sacke
3 sackes is	a surplus
104^{c} is 2 sa	208^{c} is 4 sa
416 is 8 sa	832 is 16 sa
1664^{c} is 32 sa	3328^{c} is 64 sa

Further out is a text giving values for surface measurements inscribed over both closed limbs as follows:

'A barlie corne is the least measur . yet fro<m> it do all other Procede . 3 Barlie cornes cont 1 ynche 4 in thickne<s> a fingr Bredeth . 12 ynches a foote 3 foote a yarde . 5 foote a Geometricall pace . 15 (!) fote ½ a Pearch . 20 (square) Pearc ½ a Ro . 40 (square) Pear a Roode . 80 (square) Pea ½ a Acre. 160 (square) Pea a Acre . 660 foote or 132 pace a eng furlo<n>g . 8 furlonges is a Englishe mile . 1500 pace is a french league . 1000 pace or 8 furlongs an Italian mile . 32 furlongs is a como<n> Germain mile . 253440 Barlie corns in length is an Englishe mile'.

At the bottom is a further table for calculating an acre in perches:

Acre	
Bredeth	Length
1	160
2	80
4	40
5	32
8	20
10	16

Inside of the arms

The initials of the maker 'H C' are inscribed on the inside edge at the end of one arm.

Figure 39 Detail of the Folding Gunner's rule with the signature (catalogue no. 23). Reproduced by kind permission of the Royal Artillery Historical Trust, Woolwich.

The inside edge of each arm is hollowed out and accommodates two folding tablets. The end of each tablet has a bevelled edge and a small hole to facilitate folding it out. Three of these tablets are marked on both sides.
One plate has 10 round holes of different sizes, probably to measure the size of bullets. They have the following diameters in mm:

10.9
10.2
9.9
9.4
8.8
8.5
7.8
6.9
5.8
4.6

A table giving the multiples of 44 cloves in sacks and cloves, with an 's' indicating a sack and a 'd' indicating ½ sack. The symbols for 'd' and 's' engraved on the instrument are not consistent throughout. The table is marked 'Numeratio de et d s 18^{c}' (i.e. half a sack equals 26 cloves).

1	d s 18^{c}
2	1 s d 10^{c}
3	2 s d 2^{c}
4	3 s 20^{c}
5	4 s 12^{c}
6	5 s 4^{c}
7	5 s d 22^{c}
8	6 s d 14^{c}
9	7 s d 6^{c}
10	8 s 24^{c}
11	9 s 16^{c}
12	10 s 8^{c}
13	11 s
14	11 s d 18^{c}
15	12 s d 10^{c}
16	13 s d 2^{c}
17	14 s 20^{c}
18	15 s 12^{c}
19	16 s 4^{c}
20	16 s d 22^{c}
30	25 s 20^{c}
40	33 s d 18^{c}
50	42 s 16^{c}
60	50 s d 14^{c}
70	59 s 12^{c}
80	67 s d 10^{c}
90	76 s 8^{c}
100	84 s d 6^{c}

A table giving the multiples of 9 cloves in sacks and cloves, with an 's' indicating a sack and a 'd' indicating ½ sack. The table is marked 'Allocatio 9 claue' (i.e. a multiplication of cloves in sacks and cloves to the base of 9 cloves).

1	9^{c}
2	18
3	d s 1^{c}
4	d s 10
5	d s 19
6	1 s 2^{c}
7	1 s 11^{c}
8	1 s 20^{c}
9	1 s d 3^{c}
10	1 s d 12^{c}
11	1 s d 21^{c}
12	2 s 4^{c}
13	2 s 13^{c}
14	2 s 22
15	2 s d 5^{c}
16	2 s d 14^{c}
17	2 s d 23^{c}
18	3 s 6^{c}
19	3 s 15^{c}
20	3 s 24^{c}
30	5 s 10^{c}
40	6 s d 22^{c}
50	8 s d 8^{c}
60	10 s 20^{c}
70	12 s 6^{c}
80	13 s d 18^{c}
90	15 s d 4^{c}
100	17 s 16^{c}

A table for the type of cannon, the weight of each cannon and the diameter of the barrel.

Names of ordenance	The Waight of euery Pece in Mettell	Haight in the mouthe ynches
Robinet	300	1
Fawconet	500	2
Fawcon	800	2 ¾
Mynion	1000	3
Sacar	1355	3 ½
Demicułł	2544	4 ¼
Culluerine	3021 / 4000	5 ¼
Demi Cano<n>	5700	6 ¼
Canon	6000	7 ¾
Eliza Can<o>	8000	8
	9000	8 ¾
Basilisco	12000	9

This table is continued with a table for the diameter of the bullet in inches, the powder needed for every shot in pounds, the distance where the bullet first hits the ground when fired from a horizontal barrel, in scores by paces (here mathematical paces i.e. one pace equals 5 feet), and the weight of every shot in pounds.

Haight of the Bullett ynches	The Powder that euery Pece showteth lb	Scores at Pointe blancke	Waight of every shote lb
¾	1		1
1 ¾	1 ¾	14	2
2 ½	2 ½	16	2 ½
2 ¾	4 ½	17	4 ½
3 ¼	5	18	5
4	10	20	10
5	18	25	18
6	28	28	30
7 ½	40	20	60
7 ¾	42	20	63
8 ½	60	21	60
8 ¾	60	21	90

A text for the measures of precious metal, marked 'Golde waights growith of wheate', as follows:
'32 Grains wheate is a sterling penny . 20 sterlings a oz . 12 oz a lb w^{c}z Troy . 1 lb fine (i.e. pure or '24 carat') golde is 24 Carrets (i.e. carats) w^c 24 Carrets is 24 ½(-)oz (troy) and eue{r}y Carret is divided into 24 graines w^c is called 24 carret graines and euerie of thos 24 (carat) graines is devided into 24 smale (i.e. troy) graines . 1 marke fine is xij d (here 12 penny weight) . 1 penny waight is 24 (troy) graines . 288 (troy) graines is a marke . 8 pounde waighte of wheate is a (corn) gallon . 8 (corn) gallons is a Busshell. 8 Busshelles is a quarter of wheate.'

A text for the wine measures, marked 'Wyne measures', as follows: '18 Gallons ½ is a Rondelett . 31 gallons ½ a Barrell . 63 gallons a Hogsheade . 84 gallons a Tiers . 126 gallons a pipe . 252 gallons is a Toune 2 pipes 2 Butts 4 Hogsheds 22 (symbol representing unidentified barrel name) ½ maks a Toune.

A text marked 'Phisicall waightes groweth of barlie graines', as follows: '1 Barlie corne is a graine . 20 graines is a scruple . 60 graines is a Drame . 8 Drames a ounce . 12 oz is a Pounde.'

A table for leather measures, marked 'Lether accompts', as follows: '20 Diker is a last . 10 Hides is a diker.'

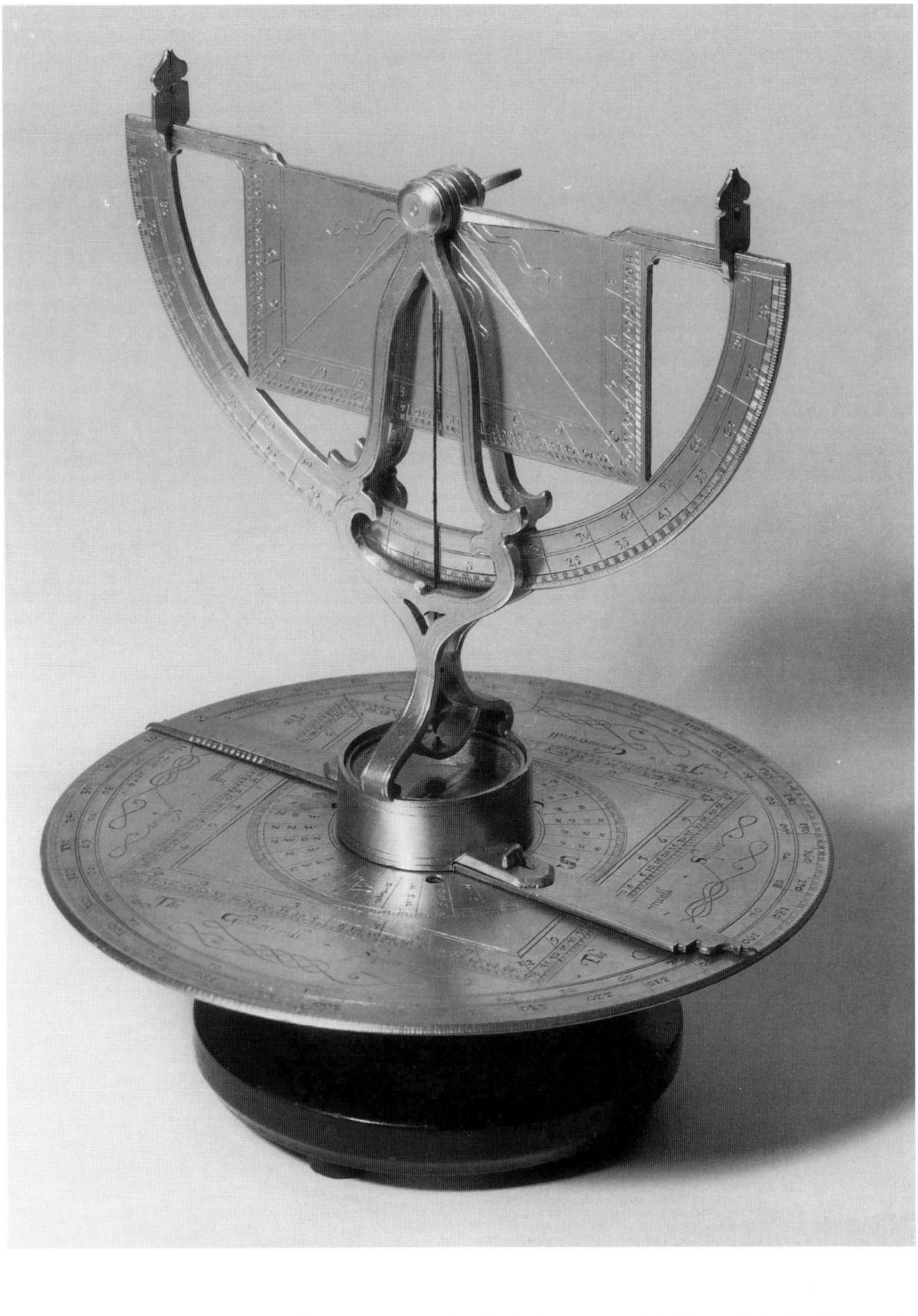

Figure 40 Altazimuth theodolite 1574 (catalogue no. 24). Reproduced by kind permission of the National Maritime Museum, London.

Altazimuth Theodolites

The urgent need for accurate surveying in the second half of the sixteenth century led to the development of the altazimuth theodolite as described by Leonard Digges in his *Pantometria*, first published in 1556. Consisting of a horizontal circle marked with a 360° scale and a geometrical square used with an alidade, and an altitude semicircle with a shadow square and sights, the instrument could be used for taking both horizontal and vertical measurements.

The two earliest surviving theodolites following this description were both made by Humphrey Cole, the theodolite in Oxford being the earliest known complete example. The instrument in Greenwich is from an earlier period, but is incomplete.

24 Altazimuth Theodolite Figure 40
National Maritime Museum, London
inv. no. NAV 1448 (previously SI/T.1)
Signed and dated: H Côle 1574
Gilt brass; maximum height 200 mm, maximum diameter 172 mm

The azimuth circle with a diameter of 172 mm is made of solid brass. The edge has a degree scale 0 - 360, numbered by 10 and divided to 5 and 1 by alternate shading. Further to the inside is another degree scale 0 - 90 - 0 - 90 - 0, numbered by 10.

Inside the degree scale is a 'Geometricall Square'. It is inscribed with two different scales: one to the base 60, numbered by 5 and divided to 1 by alternate shading, the other to the base 12, numbered by 3. The signature and the date are inscribed between the degree scale on the edge and the square as 'H Côle 1574'.

The 32 points of the compass are inscribed inside the square as 'NBE, NNE, NEBN, NE, NEBE, ENE, EBN, E' etc. with a fleur-de-lis indicating north. The scale is divided to 1/2, 1/4 and 1/8. The compass is marked with the deviation of *c.* 12° east of north.

The alidade in the length of the diameter of the azimuth circle has bevelled edges and an unnumbered degree scale on both fiducial edges, presumably 0 - 25, divided to 1 as is the scale on the Oxford instrument. This scale would correspond with the markings on the geometrical square.

The part of the instrument described as follows is a replacement.

The upper part of the instrument is attached to the alidade by screws and rotates with it, while the compass inside the bowl remains in its position once orientated. The compass bowl sits in a hollowed plate but is nevertheless detachable. The alidade is therefore allowed to rotate freely while the compass remains in a fixed position.

The altitude semicircle 172 mm in diameter, with a plumb bob attached, is fixed to a ring surrounding the compass bowl by two decorated upright supports. The ring is fixed to the alidade by two rotating lugs.

The altitude semicircle, which can be fixed at a given position by a central screw, is surmounted by two sights. It is graduated on one side with a degree scale 90 - 0 - 90, numbered by 5 and divided to 1 and ½.

The shadow square has two scales: one to the base 60, numbered by 5 and divided to 1 by alternate shading, the other to the base 12 and numbered by 3. A sun burst is engraved in the centre.

The reverse of the semicircle is left blank.

Bibliography

Turner, Gerard L'E., 'Mathematical Instrument-Making in London in the Sixteenth Century', *English Map Making 1500-1650*, ed. Sarah Tyacke (London 1983), pp. 93-106, esp. p. 102 with pl. 47.

25 Altazimuth Theodolite Figure 41
Museum of the History of Science, Oxford
inv. no. 55,130 (previously 24-37)
Signed and dated: H Cole 1586
Brass; maximum height 210 mm, maximum diameter 230 mm

Although the parts of the instrument were separated from each other in the course of history, they were reunited in the middle of this century.

The azimuth circle, with a diameter of 200 mm, consists only of a ring, not of a solid disc as in the instrument in Greenwich. It is inscribed with a degree scale 0 - 360, numbered by 10 and divided to 5 and 1.

On the same ring further to the inside, the 32 compass points are marked as 'NBE, NNE, NEBN, NE, NEBE, ENE, EBN, E' etc. North is indicated by a fleur-de-lis.

Fixed to the inside of this azimuth ring by decorative supports is a geometrical square. The signature and date are given on the support fixed to the north point of the ring as 'H Cole 1586'. The square is marked as a 'Quadratum Geometricum' and is inscribed with two different scales: one to the base 60, numbered by 5 and divided to 1, the other to the base 12, numbered by 3.

The alidade spanning the diameter of the horizontal circle, is inscribed on one edge with a scale 0 - 25, numbered by 5 and divided to 1. This scale may have corresponded to the markings on the geometrical square.

On both arms of the alidade are projections for the fitting of sights, two on the alidade and one each on protrusions outside the horizontal ring at the north and south points. All four projections are numbered by a later hand and only one original sight, numbered 2, has survived. This sight is

128 mm high and has a vertical slot with a cord in the centre.
The upper part of the instrument with the altitude semicircle is attached to the alidade by two winged screws and rotates with it, while an ingenious mechanism allows the compass to stay in a fixed position. The compass glass and needle are missing. A plumb bob is fixed to the upright support.
The semicircle is fixed with two upright supports , one of which is inscribed with the same 0 - 25 scale (numbered by 5) as the alidade. Presumably this scale was intended to be used in conjunction with the shadow square.
The semicircle (diameter 123 mm) is marked on both sides with a degree scale 90 - 0 - 90, numbered by 10 and divided to 1, and has a shadow square on the inside. The latter with a scale to the base 12 (numbered by 3 and divided to 1) is inscribed twice 'Vmbra Versa' and 'Vmbra Recta'.
The signature and date 'H Cole 1586' are inscribed on the diameter of the semicircle.
Fixed to the top of the semicircle is a bar (230 mm long) which carries a sight at each end.

Bibliography

Gunther, R.T., 'The Great Astrolabe and Other Scientific Instruments by Humphrey Cole', *Archaeologia* 76 (1927), pp. 273-317, esp. pp. 301-2.
Turner, Gerard L'E., 'Mathematical Instrument-Making in London in the Sixteenth Century', *English Map Making 1500-1650*, ed. Sarah Tyacke (London 1983), pp. 93-106, esp. p. 102 with pl. 47.

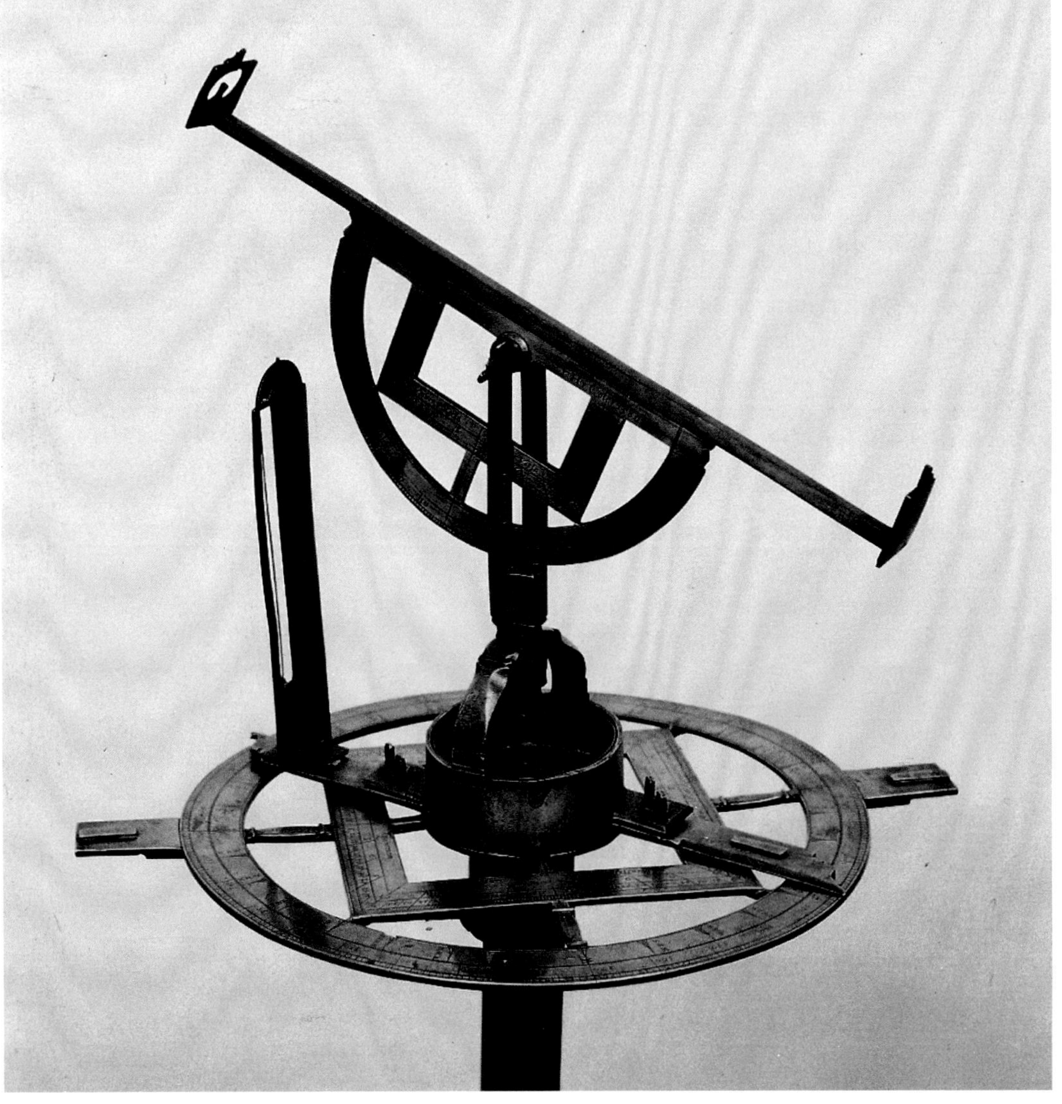

Figure 41 Altazimuth theodolite 1586 (catalogue no. 25). Reproduced by kind permission of the Museum of the History of Science, Oxford (photo Lynn Norman).

Plane Table Alidade

A plane table alidade, a rule with sighting vanes, is used in conjunction with a plane table for surveying in the field.

26 Plane Table Alidade Figure 42
Museum of the History of Science, Oxford
inv. no. 47,108 (previously 80-22)
Signed and dated: H Côle 1582
Brass; length 444 mm, width 24 mm

The instrument has the appearance of a simple rule with bevelled edges, but the two threaded holes for fixing sights make it likely that it was once used as a plane table alidade.
The rule is inscribed with two scales:
1) an inch scale 0 - 17, numbered by 1 and divided to ½, ¼ and ⅛;
2) an inch scale where every section is divided into different numbers of equal parts and marked as such. Like similar scales on the folding rules these divisions can be used in conjunction with maps.
The following divisions are given:
7 divided to 1/7.
20 divided to 1/5, 1/10, 1/20.
22 divided to 1/2, 1/11.
24 divided to 1/2, 1/4, 1/12, 1/24.
26 divided to 1/2, 1/13, 1/26.
27 divided to 1/3, 1/9, 1/27.
28 divided to 1/7, 1/14, 1/28.
30 divided to 1/3, 1/15, 1/30.
32 divided to 1/2, 1/8, 1/16, 1/32.
36 divided to 1/3, 1/9, 1/18, 1/36.
40 divided to 1/5, 1/10, 1/20, 1/40.
42 divided to 1/3, 1/21, 1/42.
48 divided to 1/12, 1/12, 1/48.
64 divided to 1/2, 1/18, 1/32, 1/64.
56 divided to 1/7, 1/14, 1/28, 1/56.
18 divided to 1/3, 1/9, 1/18.

The underside is signed and dated 'H Côle 1582'.

Bibliography

Turner, Gerard L'E., 'Mathematical Instrument-Making in London in the Sixteenth Century', *English Map-Making 1500-1650*, ed. Sarah Tyacke (London 1983), pp. 93-106, esp. pp. 102-3 with fig. 50.

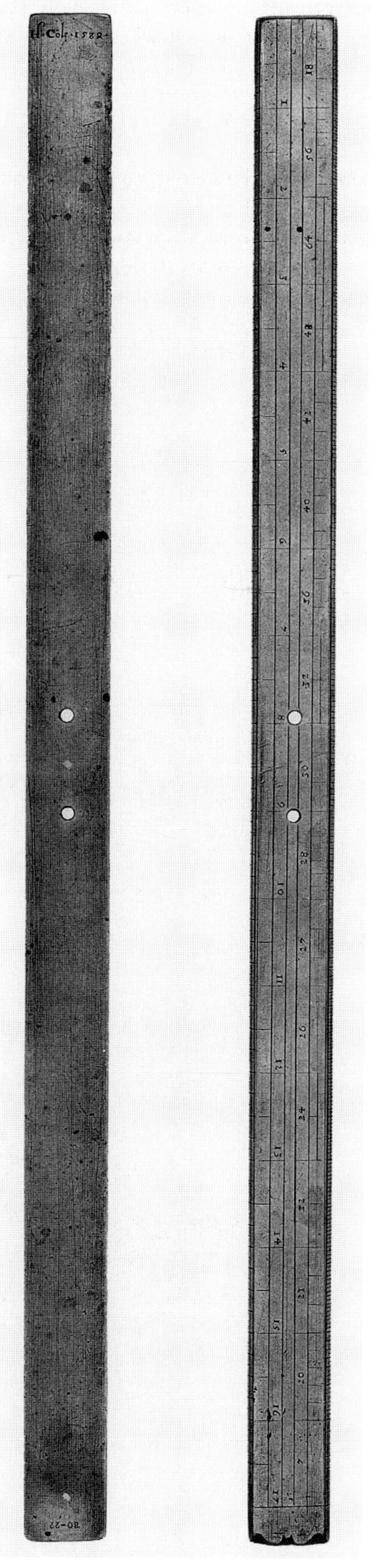

Figure 42 Plane table alidade 1582 (catalogue no. 26). Reproduced by kind permission of the Museum of the History of Science, Oxford (photo Giles Hudson).

Appendix 1
Saints' Days and Christian Feasts on Humphrey Cole's Instruments

January
1 Circumcision of Christ
6 Epiphany
13 Hilary (in England usually celebrated on 14 January, but in some continental places on 13 January)
25 Conversion of St. Paul
February
2 Purification of the Virgin Mary
14 Valentine
24 Matthew the Apostle
March
12 Gregory
25 Annunciation
April
4 Ambrose (in England usually celebrated on 7 December, but in some continental places on 4 April)
23 George
25 Mark the Evangelist
May
1 Philip and James
6 John the Evangelist
26 Augustin
June
11 Barnabas
24 John the Baptist
29 Peter and Paul
July
2 Visitation of the Virgin Mary
22 Mary Magdalen
25 James the Apostle
August
1 Peter in chains
10 Laurence
24 Bartholomew
29 Beheading of John the Baptist
September
8 Nativity of the Virgin Mary
21 Matthew the Evangelist
29 Michael
October
13 Edward the Confessor
18 Luke the Evangelist
28 Simon and Jude the Apostles
November
1 All Saints
2 All Souls
30 Andrew the Apostle
December
6 Nicholas
8 Conception of the Virgin Mary
21 Thomas the Apostle
25 Nativity of Christ

Appendix 2
Latitude list on Humphrey Cole instruments

The following locations (modernized where necessary) are given in Humphrey Cole's latitude. Note that although the values given for the latitudes are very consistent, some places are indicated with different latitudes on different instruments.

Amsterdam	52 40	Lincoln	53 15
Antwerp	51 28	Lisbon	39 0 / 39 38
Augusta (Augsburg)	47 32 / 48 0	London	51 30 / 51 33 / 51 34
Barsalo (Barcelona?)	41 35	Louvain	50 58
Barwic (Berwick)	56 0 / 56 50	Lubeck	54 48
Basingstoke	51 34	Lyons	45 0
Basileia (Basle)	48 0	Marsil (Marseille)	43 6
Bath	51 26	Middelburg	51 48
Bristowe (Bristol)	51 0 / 51 20 / 52 0	Monspessulanus (Montpellier)	42 5
Brugae (Bruges)	51 30	Nantes	48 12
Brasilia (Brussels)	51 0	Neaples	39 0 / 41 0
Cambridge	52 14 / 52 0	Newcastle	55 0
Canterbury	51 18	Northampton	52 15 / 52 50
Colchester	52 0	Norwich	52 44 / 52 30
Colonia (Cologne)	51 0	Nottingham	53 0
Compostella (Santiago de C.)	44 20	Oxford	51 47 / 51 50
Constanti (Constantinople?)	43 0	Paris	47 55
Coventry	52 28	Prague	50 4
Cracouia (Cracow)	51 0	Rome	41 50 / 42 0
Dantiseum (Danzig/Gdansk)	55 0	Rone (Rouen?)	49 0
Dover	51 0	Rouen	48 0
Edenburgh	57 0	Saulisburi (Salisbury)	51 15 / 51 34
Emden	53 42	Toledo	39 0 / 39 56
Exeter	50 45 / 51 0	Tolosa (Toulouse)	43 30
Florentia (Florence)	43 4	Tornāc (Torun)	51 40
Francophordia (Frankfurt)	50 12	Venetia (Venice)	44 50
Gandavum (Gent)	51 24	Westchester (Chester)	53 10
Harford	52 50	Winchester	51 0
Leicester	52 50	York	54 0

Glossary

Age of the moon: the moon's period of revolution between two identical phases (for example from one new moon to the next new moon), the so called 'synodic month' or 'lunation', is 29 days, 12 hours and 44 minutes. Many instruments have a lunar volvelle, a rotatable disc, with a scale of either 29 or 30 days to indicate how many days have passed since the last new moon, i.e. to indicate the age of the moon.

Alidade: a rule with sighting vanes to facilitate the readings from the scales of an astrolabe. The readings are taken against the fiducial edges, which mark the diameter of the astrolabe.

Almucantar - see 'Celestial co-ordinates'.

Altitude - see 'Celestial co-ordinates'.

Altitude sundial: a type of sundial where the time is determined by the altitude of the sun.

Armillary sphere: a skeletonised form of a celestial globe only displaying the main points and circles such as the celestial poles, the Arctic and Antarctic circles, the equator, the ecliptic and the tropics of Cancer and Capricorn etc.

Astrological houses: a division of the heavens into 12 parts for astrological purposes. There are different systems for the division, the most usual one being of Islamic origin, but commonly associated with the fifteenth-century astronomer Regiomontanus.

Azimuth - see 'Celestial co-ordinates'.

Brachiolus: Latin for 'small arm', normally jointed, with a pointer at the end. Used on the back of an astrolabe with a universal projection. See the section 'Astrolabes' in the catalogue.

Cardinal compass points - see 'Compass points'.

Celestial co-ordinates: different systems are used to denote the position of a heavenly body in the sky depending on the point of reference. All positions are measured in degrees (°), minutes (') and seconds (").
1) Horizon co-ordinates: positions are measured with reference to the horizon. A circle from the zenith to the nadir passing through a star is called an 'azimuth', denoted as A. The zero point is north.
The altitude, denoted as h, is the angle measured from the horizon along an azimuth circle. A circle of constant altitude parallel to the horizon is called an 'almucantar'.
2) Equatorial co-ordinates: positions are measured with reference to the celestial equator, i.e. the extension of the terrestrial equator into infinity. A circle drawn from the celestial North to the South Pole passing through a star is called the an 'hour circle'.
The right ascension', denoted as α, is measured eastward along the celestial equator to the hour circle. The zero point is the vernal equinox, i.e. the first point of Aries.
The angle measured along the hour circle is called the 'declination', denoted as δ.

Compass points: the cardinal points, north (N), south (S), east (E) and west (W), are subdivided to indicate finer directions. The position exactly midway between north and east for example is called 'northeast' (NE), that between north and northeast 'north by northeast' (NBNE) or 'north-northeast' (NNE).

Cursor: a rule with the length of the radius of the astrolabe to which the brachiolus is attached. See the section 'Astrolabes' in the catalogue.

Day Letter: every single day of the common year (with 365 days) is denoted with one of the seven letters A to G, starting by A for 1 January. The letter for the first Sunday of the year is called the 'Dominical Letter' and is of importance for the calculation of Easter. If for example 1 January is a Thursday, 4 January would be a Sunday. Since 1 January is A, 4 January would be D - the D being the Dominical Letter for this particular year. If the year is a leap year it has two Dominical Letters: one for the Sundays before the leap day and one for the Sundays after.

Declination - see 'Celestial co-ordinates'.

Deviation, magnetic: the difference between magnetic and true north, known to Europeans since the second half of the fifteenth century. The value for the magnetic deviation is not fixed, but changes throughout the centuries.

Dominical Letter - see 'Day Letter'.

Easter calculation: Easter is celebrated on the first Sunday after the spring full moon, where the beginning of spring itself is traditionally fixed at 21 March. To calculate Easter for a particular year, one has to know the day of the week for 21 March and the date of the full moon: therefore a combination of the solar cycle and the lunar cycle is needed. The solar cycle means that every 28 years the same date falls on the same weekday, while every 19 years (the lunar cycle) the full moon falls on the same date. While the epacts indicate the age of the moon on 22 March (the first possible Easter date), the Golden Number indicates the year of the lunar cycle.

A fixed relationship between the epacts was used throughout the centuries although the inadequacy of the Julian calendar gradually put the calendar and astronomical events out of step. The following table gives this relationship:

Epact	Golden Number
0 (or 29)	1
11	2
22	3
3	4
14	5
25	6
6	7
17	8
28	9
9	10
20	11
1	12
12	13
23	14
4	15
15	16
26	17
7	18
18	19

This relationship is always shifted by 1 on Humphrey Cole's instruments, i.e 11 equals 1, 22 equals 2 etc.

Ecliptic: the apparent annual path of the sun through the sky against the background of the stars. At the equinoxes the ecliptic crosses the celestial equator, at the solstices the sun is furthest away from the equator.

Epacts: the epacts of the Julian calendar indicate the age of the moon on 22 March. See also 'Easter calculation'.

Equal hours - see 'Hours'.

Equator: the great circle around the earth midway between the poles.

Equatorial co-ordinates - see 'Celestial co-ordinates'.

Equatorial sundial: a sundial where the hour scale is laid out on a plane parallel to the celestial equator with a gnomon pointing to the celestial North Pole. The hour scale is adjustable for different latitudes 0° - 90° thereby making the instrument universal.

Equinoxes: the two occasions in the year when the sun's path (the ecliptic) crosses the celestial equator. On these two days, the vernal and autumnal equinoxes, the length of day and night is identical.

Gnomon: Greek for the shadow caster of a sundial by which the time is indicated. The gnomon can be shaped in a multitude of different ways, such as a triangular plate on a horizontal dial, a pin on an equatorial dial or a string on a diptych dial.

Golden Number: indicates the year of the 19-year lunar cycle for a given year. The Golden Number can be calculated by the addition of 1 to the given year and the division of the result by 19. The remainder indicates the Golden Number, if the remainder is 0, the Golden Number is 19. See also 'Easter calculation'.

Gregorian calendar: the calendar introduced in 1582 and adopted gradually in Europe (with the last countries following in the beginning of the twentieth century) which brought the date back into step with astronomical phenomena, i.e. the vernal equinox back to 21 March. In England the new calendar was adopted in 1752.

Horary quadrant: an instrument (separate or a component of another instrument as for example an astrolabe) in the shape of a quarter circle with hour-lines used to indicate the time in equal or unequal hours.

Horizon - see 'Celestial co-ordinates'.

Horizon obliquus: the observer's (curved) horizon on an astrolabe plate for a particular latitude.

Horizon rectus: the horizon for an observer on the equator.

Horizontal co-ordinates - see 'Celestial co-ordinates'.

Horizontale catholicum: an astrolabe plate giving horizons for all possible latitudes thereby making the instrument's use universal.

Horse: the small wedge in the shape of a stylized horse's head, used with a pin to fix the different parts of the astrolabe to each other. See the section 'Astrolabes' in the catalogue.

Hours: while today the equal hour system is used, where the 24 hours of the day each have exactly the same length, in earlier times the unequal hour system was much more common. Here the time between sunrise and sunset, and sunset and sunrise respectively, were divided into 12 sections each, also called ' hours', but of different length each day according to the time of year except for the equinoxes, when they are equal.

Julian calendar: the calendar introduced by Julius Caesar in 46 BC and used until the introduction of the Gregorian calendar in 1582. Due to an inappropriate use of leap days the calendar became more and more out of step with astronomical phenomena so that the date for the spring equinox had moved away from the 21 March towards the beginning of March - in Humphrey Cole's time being 10 or 11 March.

Latitude - see 'Terrestrial co-ordinates'.

Linea crepusculi: a curve found on some astrolabe plates indicating the beginning and end of (astronomical) twilight, i.e. when the sun is 18° below the horizon.

Longitude - see 'Terrestrial co-ordinates'.

Lunar volvelle - see 'Age of the moon'.

Mater: part of the astrolabe. See the catalogue entry 'Astrolabes'.

Meridian: a great circle passing through the North and South Poles and intersecting the equator.

Month names in Latin: Ianuarius, Februarius, Martius, Aprilis, Maius, Iunius, Iulius, Augustus, September, October, November, December.

Nadir: the point on the celestial sphere directly below one's feet.

Planetary symbols: the symbols used to denote the seven planets, i.e. Moon, Mercury, Venus, Sun, Mars, Iupiter, Saturn.

☾ ☿ ♀ ☉ ♂ ♃ ♄

Planetary temperaments: a system used by the Greek astronomer Ptolemy in the second century in his *Tetrabiblos* book I, ch. 9, according to which each planet exerts some influence on a particular star.

Plate: component of an astrolabe. See the section 'Astrolabes' in the catalogue.

Pointer stars: the two prominent stars α and β of the constellation Ursa Maior (Great Bear) which align with the Pole Star.

Prime meridian - see 'Terrestrial co-ordinates'.

Right ascension - see 'Celestial co-ordinates'.

Quadratum nauticum: a graduated square frequently found on Flemish and Flemish-influenced instruments which allows the sailor to find, without calculation, the course between two points of which the latitude and longitude are known.

Rete: Latin for 'web' or 'net'. The celestial part of the astrolabe, see the section 'Astrolabes' in the catalogue.

Solstices: the dates in June and December when the sun's path reaches maximum distance from the equator and the longest and shortest days respectively occur.

Star names with magnitudes: following Ptolemy's definition in books VII and VIII of his *Almagest* the stars are classified according to their brightness, 1 indicating the most prominent stars, and 6 the faintest star which can be seen with the naked eye.

Star-pointer: a protrusion of different shape on the rete, the celestial part of the astrolabe, indicating the position of a star. See the section 'Astrolabes' in the catalogue.

Throne: part of the astrolabe. See the section 'Astrolabes' in the catalogue.

Terrestrial co-ordinates: the terrestrial co-ordinates are called 'longitude' and 'latitude' and the signs to denote these are λ and φ.
Longitude is an arc measured along the equator with an arbitrarily chosen zero point, called the prime meridian. Since 1884 the meridian of Greenwich is accepted as the prime meridian, but before this time different prime meridians were in use, with Ptolemy's Fortunate Islands being the most common one in Humphrey Cole's time.
Latitude is measured north and south of the equator along a meridian.
Longitude and latitude are measured in degrees (°), minutes (') and seconds (").

Tropics: the circles in the sky parallel to the celestial equator, indicating the extreme positions of the sun during the solstices. The circle north of the equator is the 'Tropic of Cancer', the one south of the equator the 'Tropic of Capricorn', thus indicating the zodiacal sign through which the sun is passing at the time.

Unequal hours - see 'Hours'.

Zenith: the point on the celestial sphere directly overhead.

Zodiac: the belt around the sky in which the Sun, Moon and principal planets are to be found, since Antiquity conventionally divided into 12 regions or 'signs' of 30° each, named after the constellation to be found in this section of the sky. The Latin names of the signs and their symbols used are:

Aries	♈	Taurus	♉
Gemini	♊	Cancer	♋
Leo	♌	Virgo	♍
Libra	♎	Scorpio	♏
Sagittarius	♐	Capricorn	♑
Aquarius	♒	Pisces	♓

Humphrey Cole's Map of Palestine

Peter Barber

27 Map of Palestine Figure 43
British Library, London
469.g.8

Cole's map shows the Holy Land, divided into the areas occupied by the sons of Cham and marks the route of the Exodus.

This, Cole's sole known map, is generally found bound into copies of the second edition (1572) of the *Bishop's Bible* which had originally appeared, sponsored by Archbishop Matthew Parker, in 1568. The 1572 edition contained four other woodcut maps and it is likely that the map was an after-thought and optional addition. It was probably commissioned by the Bible's publisher, Richard Jugge, who had been associated with Cole since at least 1568 and whose badge is to be seen on the right side of the map. Nevertheless, there are copies of the 1572 Bible that never seem to have contained this map and it is not to be found in any of the numerous later editions of the Bible printed by Jugge.[1]

The map itself is the same size as, and is very closely copied from, a map of the same area by Abraham Ortelius (Abraham Ortels), even down to the positioning and word breaks of the names of the tribes and provinces. Ortelius' map (Figure 44) had first been published in Antwerp in May 1570 as part of his *Theatrum Orbis Terrarum*, the first modern atlas. The *Theatrum* rapidly became a standard source for other map engravers and publishers because of the high quality of Ortelius's editing and because of its enormous print-run by the standards of the time.[2] In its turn Ortelius' map, as he acknowledged, had been copied from a map by the German cartographer Tilleman Stella (Stoltz) that had first appeared in 1557.[3] It formed part of a tradition of mapping of Palestine that dated back to Roman times.[4]

There are, however, two significant differences between Cole's map and its prototype.[5] On Cole's map many (though not all) of the inscriptions and provincial and place names are translated into English (he also adds the statement above the scale bar, which does not include English miles, that 'the Italian and English miles are egall viz. a 1000 paces'). Secondly he has added thumbnail depictions, reminiscent of details from medieval *mappae mundi*, of episodes that occurred in the course of the Exodus, such as the worship of the Golden Calf. It was a characteristic of protestant Bibles to be written in the vernacular and to include visual aids such as maps and illustrations within maps so as to emphasise the literal truth of scripture and to make the Bible's contents understandable to the common man.[6] Taken with the historical text contained in the lengthy title, the map could have stood alone as a teaching aid, independently of the Bible into which it was bound.

The use of English reflects the patriotism that was characteristic of Elizabethan England. This finds further expression in the panel inserted in place of the privilege statement on Ortelius's map, that the map had been 'Graven bi Humfray Cole goldsmith an English man born in ye north and pertayning to ye mint in the Tower 1572', (see Figure 45).

The arms of Lord Burghley, Elizabeth I's Lord Treasurer and most important minister, suggest that he supported the map's creation in some way. He had been involved with the *Bishop's Bible* since its inception. It is, however, perhaps more likely that, far from being actively involved, the arms and the unusually lengthy authorial inscription[7] were intended to attract Burghley and bring the map to his attention, with Cole or Jugge meeting such production costs as there were. Given his position in the Mint, Cole would have had easy access to engraving tools and metal. Since the map was a close copy of another printed map, no research would have been necessary, leaving only his time to be charged for.

Cole would have had good reason for seeking Burghley's favour. Quite apart from the patronage at his disposal by virtue of the office he held, the Lord Treasurer was particularly enthusiastic about maps.[8] It may be that Cole intended to display his ability as a map engraver at a time when he knew that such skills were likely to be in demand for the detailed maps of England and Wales that Burghley wished to see commissioned and was prepared to support with government money.[9] It is striking, in this context, that in his authorship statement Cole implicitly disclaims any responsibility for the intellectual content of the map, stating simply that he had engraved it. His virtuosity is displayed on the map in the roman and italic lettering, the ships, the cartouche, the arms, the sea monster and the miniature scenes.

It has been said that the plate for this map was engraved on silver.[10] This may not be far-fetched since the antiquary, John Leland, had talked of engraving a map of England on silver for Henry VIII[11] and the importance of the subject-matter may have justified such a high quality engraving surface. Because of his work at the Mint, Cole would have had no difficulty in finding the silver.

Notes

1 Catherine Delano Smith and Elizabeth Morley Ingram, *Maps in Bibles 1500-1600* (Geneva 1991), pp. 60-61 (Cole's map described under 3.5); 149 (E1572) and ill. 35; Arthur H. Hind, *Engraving in England in the Sixteenth & Seventeenth Centuries. Part 1: The Tudor Period* (Cambridge 1952), pp 79-80.

2 Marcel P.R. van den Broecke *Ortelius Atlas Maps: An Illustrated Guide* (Westrenen 1996), p. 221 no. 170 gives the most up-to-date information and bibliography. The 1570 map is the first of at least three states. It was republished twice in 1571 and three times in 1572. Van den Broecke estimates that 1,675 copies of this first state were printed before 1575.

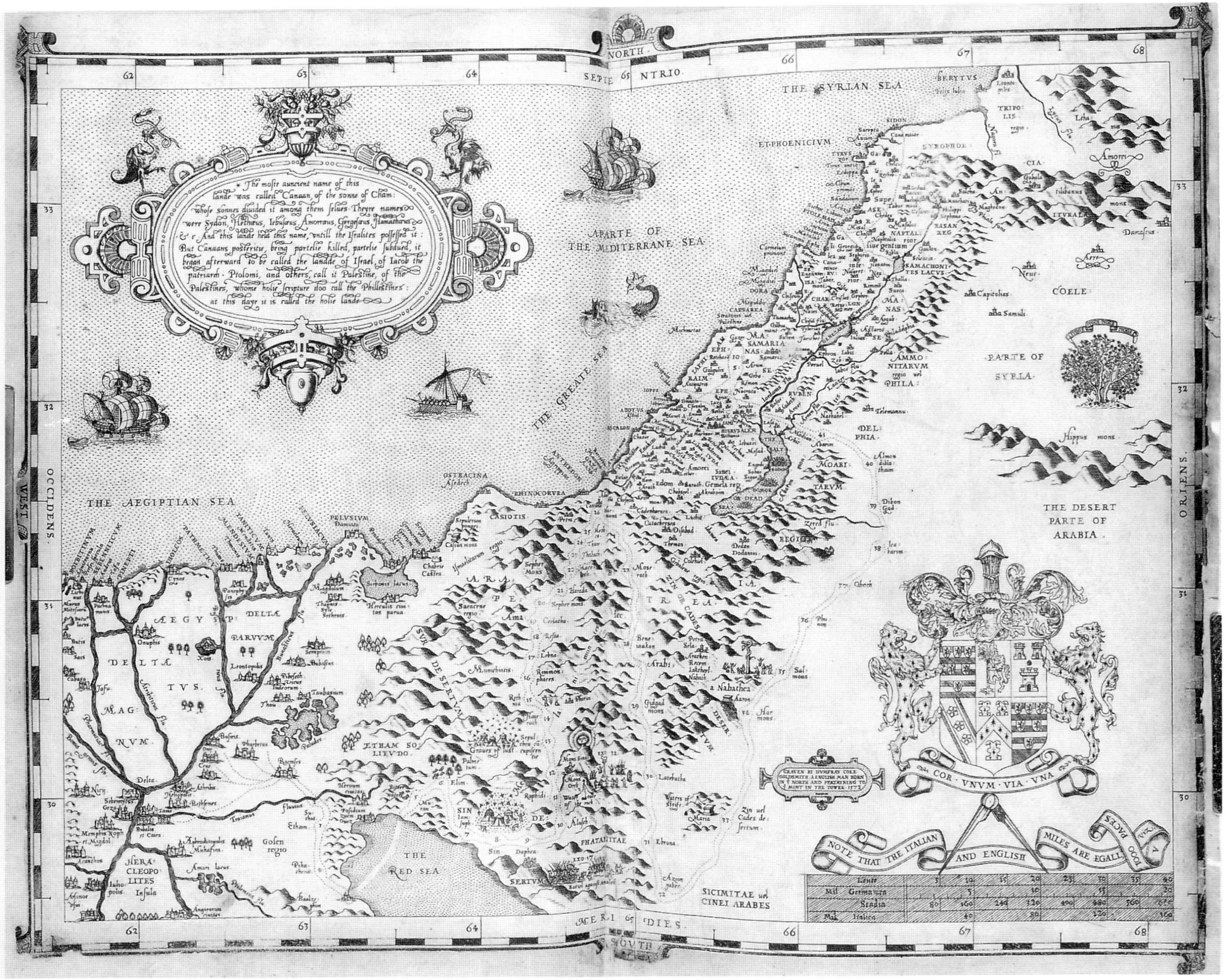

Figure 43 *Humphrey Cole, 'Canaan . . . at this daye . . . called the holie lande'. London: Richard Jugge, 1572 (British Library 469.g.8) (catalogue no. 27). Reproduced by kind permission of the British Library.*

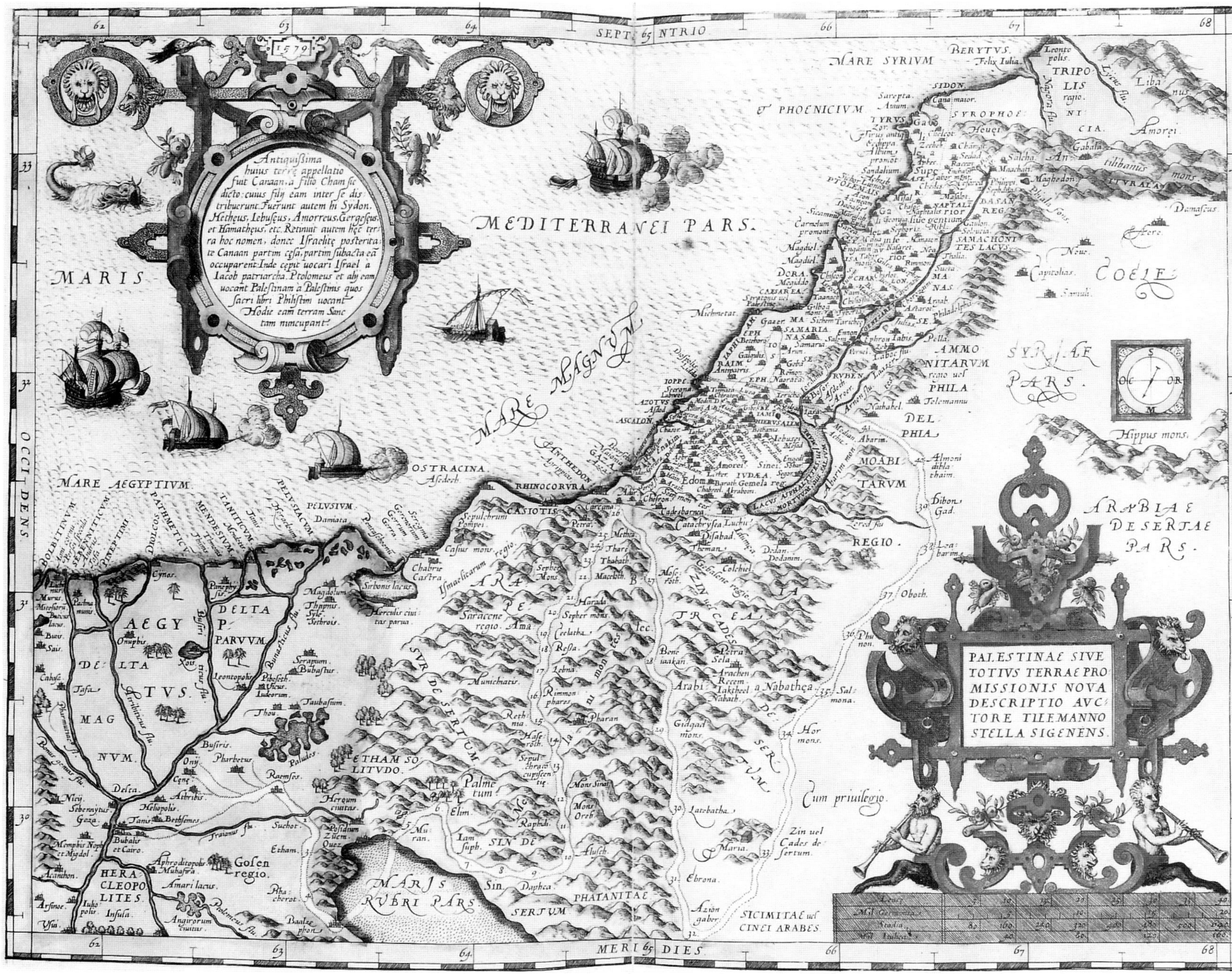

Figure 44 *Map of Palestine published by Ortelius in his Theatrum Orbis Terrarum, 1570 (British Library, Maps). Reproduced by kind permission of the British Library.*

[3] Robert Karrow, *Mapmakers of the Sixteenth Century and Their Maps* (Chicago 1993), pp. 502-3.

[4] P.D.A. Harvey, 'Local and Regional Cartography in Medieval Europe', *The History of Cartography. Volume 1: Cartography in Prehistoric, Ancient and Medieval Europe and the Mediterranean*, ed. by J.B. Harley and David Woodward, (Chicago 1987) , pp. 473-6. For an illustrated survey: Kenneth Nebenzahl, *Maps of the Bible Lands* (London 1986).

[5] Cole's map differs from Ortelius's in several minor ways. It has a different title and title cartouche (almost certainly copied from a pattern-book printed in Flanders). There are small differences in the decorations (for instance in the number of ships depicted), and it contains the arms of William Cecil who in that year had been created Lord High Treasurer and had been elevated to the peerage as Lord Burghley.

[6] See Delano Smith and Ingram, p. xvi; Catherine Delano Smith, 'Maps as Art *and* Science: Maps in Sixteenth Century Bibles', *Imago Mundi* 42 (1990), pp. 65-83.

[7] Normally the name of the engraver would have sufficed. There is some analogy in the map of England, Wales and Ireland (now BL Add. Ms 62540) that Laurence Nowell presented to Burghley in 1564 which contains not simply the name but an actual portrait of Nowell (and see P.M. Barber, 'A Tudor Mystery: Laurence Nowell's Map of England and Ireland', *The Map Collector* 22 (March 1983), pp. 16-21). In 1661, in an attempt to be re-instated as Chief Engraver to the Mint, the engraver Thomas Simon produced a crown-sized trial piece for Charles II and in addition to placing his initials under the bust, he fitted the wording of a short petition criticising his competitor's work onto the edge! Cole's inscription would, of course, have advertised his skills to *all* readers of the Bible. By the early eighteenth century, the map publisher George Willdey was using his maps to advertise the wares available from his shop, including watches, clocks. microscopes, pistols, combs and razors, all of which were illustrated (see Rodney Shirley, *Printed Maps of the British Isles 1650-1750* (London 1988), pp. 152-3).

[8] See particularly R.A. Skelton and J. Summerson, *A Description of Maps and Architectural Drawings in the Collection Made by William Cecil, First Baron Burghley, Now at Hatfield House* (Oxford 1971); Peter Barber, 'England II: Monarchs, Ministers and Maps, 1550-1625', *Monarchs Ministers and Maps. The emergence of Cartography as a Tool of Government in Early Modern Europe*, ed by D. Buisseret (Chicago 1992), pp. 69-77.

[9] This was to result in the creation of Christopher Saxton's county maps which appeared from 1574. See P.M. Barber, 'Les Iles Britanniques', *Gerardi Mercatoris Atlas Europae*, ed. Marcel Watelet (Antwerp, 1994), particularly pp. 66-72; William Ravenhill, *Christopher Saxton's 16th Century Maps* (Shrewsbury 1992), pp. 9-20 and its brief but up-to-date bibliography. It is likely that Cole knew Saxton or his master, John Rudd, both of whom were, like Cole, from the north of England.

[10] Vertue's notebooks, BL Add. Ms 23078, f. 11 cited by Arthur H. Hind, p. 80.

[11] John Leland, *The Laboriouse Journey and Serche of Johan Lelande for Englandes Antiquitees* (London, 1549).

Figure 45 Detail of Humphrey Cole's Map of Palestine. London: Richard Jugge, 1572 (British Library 469.g.8) (catalogue no. 27). Reproduced by kind permission of the British Library.

Coinage of Elizabeth I
Produced during Humphrey Cole's Tenure at the Mint (*c.* 1563-*c.*1578)

Barrie Cook

28 (1-19) Coins Figure 46 (1-19)
British Museum, London

Gold coinage

Gold coinage in the early years of Elizabeth I was produced to two standards, 'angel gold', the virtually pure medieval standard; and 'crown gold' of 22 carats, introduced under Henry VIII. The same denomination could be filled by coins of the two standards: e.g. the half-pound and the slightly lighter, though finer, angel were both 10-shilling coins. In the 1560s crown gold dominated, but after 1571 there was an almost total shift to angel gold for the next decade.

1. **Gold half-pound** (10 shillings), initial mark castle (1570-2)
CM 1895,3-1,41

2. **Gold crown** (5 shillings), im portcullis (1565/6-66/7)
CM 1920,8-16,158 Presented by the Goldsmiths' Company

3. **Gold half-crown** (2s.6d.), im lion (1566/7-67)
CM 1841,7-30,21

4. **Gold angel** (10 shillings), im eglantine (1574-8)
CM Grueber 493

5. **Gold half-angel** (5 shillings), im ermine (1572-3)
CM 1896,12-2,11

6. **Gold quarter-angel** (2s.6d), im ermine (1572-3)
CM 1896,12-2,12

Silver coinage

All the silver coinage of Elizabeth's reign was of the traditional sterling standard, used since at least the twelfth century, before overthrown by Henry VIII's debasement policies. During the recoinage period of 1560-1, huge numbers of shillings were produced, and the output of this denomination then ceased until the 1580s. The new denominations of three-halfpence and three-farthings were intended to ameliorate the shortage of small change, since good silver halfpennies and farthings had become too small to be conveniently manufactured and handled. Some of the coins here illustrated demonstrate the work of the die-sinker in altering useable dies.

7. **Silver sixpence**, im pheon (1561-5), dated 1563
The date has been changed from 1562 to 1563, by an overstamp of the last numeral.
CM 1935,4-1,2169 T.B. Clarke-Thornhill Bequest

8. **Silver sixpence**, im pheon, dated 1564
The date has been changed from 1563 to 1564.
CM 1913,12-4, Lady Ramsey Bequest

9. **Silver sixpence**, im lion (1566/7-67), no date
The date on the reverse has been mistakenly omitted.
CM 1851,2-28,5

10. **Silver sixpence**, im castle (1570-2), dated 1569
The incorrect date has been left unchanged, but the im castle is stamped over im coronet (1567-70).
CM 1933,2-1,2 from the Elland Treasure Trove

11. **Silver sixpence**, im eglantine (1574-8), dated 1577
The date 1576 has been changed to 1577.
CM E0444

12. **Silver threepence**, im coronet (1567-70), dated 1578
The rose which should be behind the queen's head has been omitted.
CM 1946,10-4,429 Oldroyd Bequest

13. **Silver threepence**, im ermine (1573-4), dated 1572
An incorrect date has been used with a later initial mark.
CM E0558

14. **Silver half-groat** (twopence), im crown (1567-70)
CM E0585

15. **Silver three-halfpence**, im ermine (1572-3), dated 1572
CM E0607

16. **Silver penny**, im coronet (1567-70)
CM 1935,4-1,2372 T.B. Clarke-Thornhill Bequest

17. **Silver three-farthings**, im acorn (1573-4), dated 1573
CM 1877,4-2,10 Houghton Treasure Trove

Coinage of Eloy Mestrell

These sixpences were produced on Eloy Mestrell's mechanised presses. Their superiority of appearance to hand-struck coin is evident, but trials held at the mint, before the hostile eyes of the traditional moneyers, showed his techniques to be slower in producing coin to the correct weight standard. Number 19, with its retrograde Ns, illustrated the limitations of the letter font Mestrell was using in the late 1560s.

18. **Silver sixpence**, milled coinage, im star (1560-66/7), dated 1566
CM Bank Collection M114 Given by the Bank of England

19. **Silver sixpence**, milled coinage, im lis (1566/7-70), dated 1570
CM E0526

Figure 46 (1-19) Coinage of Elizabeth I produced during Humphrey Cole's tenure at the mint (c. 1563-c. 1578) (catalogue no. 28).

Numismatic Glossary

Eglantine - See initial mark

Ermine - See initial mark

Initial mark/im - On English medieval and early modern coinage, the shape or symbol placed at the start of the legend, usually on both sides of the coin. Its purpose was to help safeguard standards of weight and fineness. During the use of each mark, a quantity of coin was extracted at random to be checked subsequently by weighing and assay in the Trial of the Pyx. From the point of view of the mint, it was the initial mark which defined each issue. The shapes used were usually fairly simple, and on Elizabeth I's coinage, included a castle, coronet, star and lion. Other initial marks were the pheon (an arrowhead shape), eglantine (a flower-head), ermine (derived from the stylised heraldic ermine's tail), and lis, or fleur-de-lis (a stylised lily).

£sd - English coinage in the early modern period used the £sd system: the pound (£) of 20 shillings (s.); and shilling of 12 pence (d.). There were two halfpence to 1d, and four farthings to 1d.

Legend - The inscription on a coin or medal.

Letter font - In coinage, a set of punches for producing legends with letters of the same size and style.

Lis - See initial mark.

Milled coinage - Coinage produced using mechanised techniques of manufacture. The term normally refers to early methods in use in the sixteenth and seventeenth century.

Pheon - See initial mark.

Sterling - Standard of fineness of the English silver coinage in use since at least the twelfth century. Sterling silver consists of 92.5% fine metal.

English Standard Troy Weight Verified at the Mint, 1588

Allen Simpson

29 English Standard Troy Weight Figures 47, 48
National Museums of Scotland, Edinburgh
inv. no. T.1997.29

The first widespread issues of standard weights and measures to the principal towns of England and Scotland came in the second half of the sixteenth century. The most exacting metrological work was traditionally conducted at national mints, where the best contemporary technicians were employed by the monarch to control the weight and fineness of coin. In England, a number of official enquiries in Elizabeth's reign culminated in a weight issue in 1588 when the modern levels of the troy (bullion) and avoirdupois (heavy goods) weight series were finally established.[1] These were duplicated from new standards constructed in 1582 for the Exchequer under the supervision of William, Lord Burghley, Elizabeth's Lord Treasurer. A new linear standard for the Exchequer was also made in 1588, but physical capacity standards to replace those of 1497 were not produced until 1601 (although in practice trading standards were probably verified against linear dimensions). In Scotland, an equivalent assize of weights and measures of 1587 legalised new national standards provided by Archibald Napier, General of the Scottish Mint.[2] Mint assay-masters and weight makers continued to dominate precision legal metrology during official enquiries in the mid-eighteenth and early nineteenth centuries, and the Mint's close involvement in such work provides an essential context for Cole's own work.[3]

Fifty-seven sets of the 1588 English avoirdupois and troy weight were stamped as verified at the Exchequer: they were distributed to the principal English towns, but a set was also retained at the Exchequer, and others were sent to the Goldsmiths' Company in London and to the Mint, in the Tower of London. Other towns were able to purchase further reference sets, but the only one at present known from the literature is the one issued from the Tower to Aldeburgh in Suffolk, and there are grounds for believing that all the 1588 standards were adjusted at the Tower.[4] This highly decorated 128-ounce standard cup weight is from the Aldeburgh troy set, and it would originally have contained a nest of 11 other weights from 64 ounces down to an eighth of an ounce. It has been badly damaged - perhaps to signify that it was no longer to be used as a standard after the set's replacement by more accurate Imperial standards in the 1820s.

This is a rare survival of an official weight stamped (inside and on the base) with the 'Tower' mark to show its adjustment at the Mint, which must have distributed very many such standards. The base is also marked with a crowned 'EL', to signify the 1588 issue (earlier issues were marked with a crowned 'E'), and with the marks for both the troy and avoirdupois series, together with the 'rose' mark of the English Mint.[5] For some reason which is not entirely clear, but which probably resulted from the Mint's practice of conservative adjustment against their existing coinage standards, the 1588 weights have been adjusted down to a level which is fractionally above (by about 3 grains in a pound of 5,760 grains) that of the 1582 Exchequer prototypes on which they are ostensibly based, and which in turn were derived from the earlier standards of the Goldsmith's Company.[6] At least one other 'heavy' set of 1588 troy standards at the Mint was recorded in 1758 as carrying the 'Tower' stamp.[7]

Notes

1 For papers relating to these Elizabethan enquiries see W.H. Chisholm, *Seventh Report of the Warden of the Standards* (London 1873), pp. 11-15, and 'Report from the Committee [chaired by Sir John Proby, first Baron Carysfort], appointed to inquire into the Original Standards of Weights and Measures in this Kingdom, and to consider the Laws relating thereto, 26 May 1758', *Reports from Committees of the House of Commons* (1737-65), II, pp. 443-448.

2 T. Thomson and C. Innes (eds.), *The Acts of the Parliaments of Scotland*, 13 vols. (Edinburgh 1814-76), III, pp. 521-522. The assize is discussed in R.D. Connor and A.D.C. Simpson, *The Weights and Measures of Scotland* (forthcoming).

3 Discussed in A.D.C. Simpson and R.D. Connor, 'The Mass of the English Troy Pound in the Eighteenth Century' (forthcoming).

4 The 64-ounce weight from Aldeburgh troy set was recorded in a public enquiry to Ipswich Museum in 1973 (although the 'Tower' mark was not noted): [M. Stevenson], 'Aldeburgh Troy Weight of 1588', *Libra*, 10 (1972-4), pp. 74-75. The National Museums of Scotland also have the standard 1-pound weight from the 1588 Aldeburgh avoirdupois set (Inv. T.1997.38).

5 For the identification of the 'rose' mark, see [G. Graham], 'An Account of a Comparison lately made by some Gentlemen of the Royal Society, of ... several Weights lately made for their use, with Original Standards in ... the Tower, &c', *Philosophical Transactions*, 42 (1742-3), p. 555. The crowned 'rose' and 'thistle' marks, the latter for the Scottish Mint, are present on the surviving 1687 troy standards of the Edinburgh Mint: see Connor and Simpson, note (2), above.

6 Discussed in Simpson and Connor, note (3), above.

7 Carysfort, note (1), p. 437.

Figure 47 *English standard troy weight verified at the mint 1588 (catalogue no. 29). Reproduced by kind permission of the Trustees of the National Museums of Scotland.*

Figure 48 *The Tower stamp on the English standard troy weight (catalogue no. 29). Reproduced by kind permission of the Trustees of the National Museums of Scotland.*